THE WELL-TEMPERED LISTENER

THE WELL-TEMPERED LISTENER

Growing Up with Musical Parents

HEALEY WILLAN
ELLEN WILLAN

MARY WILLAN MASON

Words Indeed Publishing Inc., Toronto
wordsindeed@rogers.com

ISBN: 978-0-9865-1660-3

Printed in Canada on acid-free paper

Library and Archives Canada Cataloguing in Publication

Mason, Mary Willan
The well-tempered listener : growing up with musical parents / Mary Willan Mason.

Includes index.
ISBN 978-0-9865-1660-3

1. Willan, Healey, 1880-1968. 2. Willan, Gladys, 1883-1964.
3. Mason, Mary Willan. 4. Musicians – Ontario – Toronto – Biography.
5. Toronto (Ont.) – Biography. I. Title.

ML410.W712W72 2010 780.92 C2010-900228-8

PHOTOGRAPHS:
Page 19: Mary Willan at Thompson's Bush on Lake Ontario, c. 1925.
Page 85: Mary Willan with Nicky in garden at 139 Inglewood Drive – apple tree in background, c. 1937.
Page 113: Front cover of Gladys Willan, *A Manual of Ear-training and Sight-singing* (Toronto: Frederick Harris Music Co. 1939), reprint.
Page 169: Healey Willan at organ, St Mary Magdalene's Church (photo: Donald McKay).

Design: Val Cooke

To Professor N.J. Endicott,
who greeted me a few years after I graduated:
"Don't remember your name, but you're the girl who can write!
What are you doing?"
I told him I was collecting rejection slips,
and he replied: "GOOD! Keep it up."

Contents

THE WELL-TEMPERED LISTENER

Prelude:
More Reminiscences about Toronto?

Is it appropriate to offer readers another volume of reminiscences about Toronto? Aren't there enough of them already? That I should think of adding to the flood was a suggestion that I first received from Lois Weir in 1994, when she was assistant dean of the Faculty of Music at the University of Toronto.

The Opera School in the faculty was about to present *Les Mamelles de Tirésias* by Francis Poulenc. Was I planning to go? Had I ever heard of Francis Poulenc? Well, I could answer "Yes" to both questions. I informed Lois that I had indeed heard of Poulenc. He and his very close friend Pierre Bernac, the foremost interpreter of his songs, performed in Toronto shortly after the Second World War. I told Lois that Mother and I were at the recital that the Women's Musical Club produced and afterwards attended a tea party with the composer, the soloist, and the club's executive.

I was sitting next to Francis Poulenc in the Round Room atop Eaton's College Street store. Pierre Bernac, sitting on the other side of him, seemed to get quite a charge out of our conversation. Since I was less than half the age of any of the women present and, I believe, considered comely in my youth, Francis proceeded to make the party most agreeable for both of us, ignoring everyone else, to Pierre's obvious amusement.

I thought it my duty to say something to the great composer, so I told him that I had enjoyed the recital very much.

"Which song did you like best?" Francis asked me.

I said I particularly liked the animal songs, his settings of Apollinaire's poems.

"Which one of those did you like best?" he asked me.

I replied I liked them all and couldn't settle on just one. Then Francis talked about his student days at the Paris Conservatoire and the day he was to give a student recital. He included a composition of his own, and there was a young lady whom he admired and whom he wanted very much to come and hear him play it.

"She said she would," and his voice saddened, "but she wasn't there."

He said he asked her why she didn't come when he had asked her so specially. Her answer was that she wanted to go shopping to buy a green hat.

Francis took my hand in both of his and, with a gentle expression in his eyes, inquired softly, "You wouldn't have done that, would you?"

I said the first thing that popped into my head, "Absolutely not!" Francis gave my hand a little squeeze and said, "I thought not."

Yes, I have heard of Francis Poulenc, I told Lois Weir, and when I listen to his music I can still discern the particular timbre and rhythm of his voice. Then you must write a book about your memories, Lois suggested. Here she was, talking to someone who had actually chatted with Francis Poulenc.

"Write a book," she said again, licking her lips.

I am not a musician, so my recollections are those of a child who was growing up with a father *and a mother* who thought, slept, produced, and performed music through the 'Jazz Age' of the 1920s, the Great Depression, the Second World War, and beyond. As an adult I observed them too as their long and remarkable personal and musical relationship continued to develop.

My mother, Gladys ('Nell') Hall, was a superb pianist and singer, a gold medallist of the Royal Academy of Music in London, England, and ordinary conversation between my parents often included words such as 'andante,' 'faux bourdon,' 'largo,' 'presto,' and 'tempi' and references to J.S. Bach's *The Well-Tempered Clavichord*. I was about four years old, I think, when I started to tire of well-intentioned souls asking if I were musical and what instrument I played. I figured that I needed a standard answer ready. So the next questioner heard it.

"Are you musical, dear? And what do you play?"

"I'm the well-tempered listener." That line received such a big laugh that I have used it ever since.

My three brothers and I never became proficient at any musical instrument, although, thanks largely to my parents, I am knowledgeable about and love music and even worked for a few years as a music critic. When in the early 1930s drawing began to fascinate me and occupy my time, Dad told me that if I preferred that to practising piano I should follow my instincts.

Composer Godfrey Ridout, a former pupil of Dad's, once told me in all seriousness that my father was not, as he put it, a family man.

"Were you there, Godfrey?" I countered. Dad may not have been at home as much as most fathers, but, when he was, he was very much a father, willing to discuss anything at all that any of us children had in mind and treating us with the dignity of an adult. And Mother was the same.

For my parents, 139 Inglewood Drive, near Yonge Street and St Clair Avenue in then-northern Toronto, became home within weeks of my birth in July 1920 and remained so for the rest of their long lives. Here's what I heard – and observed – at home

CHAPTER ONE

Mother, Dad, and the Boys

Her heart sank, so Mother told me years later. The taxi turned left as it moved south on Inglewood Drive from St Clair Avenue, passing two or three mansions set in pleasant grounds and a few attractive centre hall–plan homes. Then it pulled up at 139, the ugliest old placc on the street, a three-storey, red-brick farmhouse, vernacular all right, but that was too kind a word for its utter lack of charm or design. The inside was as fearsomely awful as the outside, but it served as home to Healey and 'Nell' Willan for the rest of their long lives. Mother accepted it with her usual grace, but I don't think she ever reconciled herself to her fate. In 1920, she had been in Canada six years and still found the local customs curious, even incomprehensible.

'Gladys,' Mother's real name, she disliked, and so she used her second name, Ellen, which she shortened to 'Nell.' She had grown up in the Forest Gate area of London, England, in a family of three boys and two girls. Her parents expected all of them to be musical. Her father, Edward Valentine Hall, played the violin and in the garden shed wrote music for his own enjoyment. As each son was born, Grandfather automatically added him to the family string section.

The oldest boy, John Beaumont, wanted to spend his life painting, but Grandfather had other plans. He shipped Uncle Jack as a young man off to Berlin to study at the Hochschule with the fabulous violinist Joseph Joachim, the close friend of Brahms's and champion of his music. My uncle's studies ended abruptly when, according to Mother, he was sauntering along Unter den Linden and a Prussian officer with sword, boots, and spurs knocked over a pregnant woman and kept on going. Her brother let the fellow know how he felt about such behaviour. Fortunately a friend of Grandfather's was passing in his carriage and witnessed the whole affair. He cabled Edward Hall to summon his son home immediately. As Mother put it, her brother wasn't long in Berlin, but long enough to acquire a superb bowing arm from the greatest master of the violin. He wound up serving as concertmaster of the Crystal Palace Symphony and painting gentle water-colour landscapes in his spare time.

After Grandfather Hall had established his own string quartet with himself and the three boys, Mother arrived March 19, 1883, and in due course she enlarged the group into a piano quintet. Later she went to the Royal Academy of Music to study piano, and she added voice. She was a year ahead of Dame Myra Hess, who distinguished herself throughout the Second World War playing noon-hour recitals, 'brown baggers,' in central London for people working there. Even the Luftwaffe and their bombs could not stop that lady. Mother and Dame Myra had the same teachers, Tobias Matthay and Francesco Berger, the two top-rated instructors. Each graduated with the coveted red silk scarf – I still have my mother's – and gold medals.

But Nell Hall received an additional honour. As Dad told me, one afternoon shortly before graduation she received a summons to the office of Sir Alexander Mackenzie, principal of the Academy and conductor of the London Philharmonic. He had a problem: unforeseen circumstances were delaying that evening's soloist in France. The performer had missed the rehearsal, as bad weather in the English Channel had forced cancellation of the ferry crossing. Sir Alexander said: "You know the Tchaikowsky No. 2. There is no time for rehearsal, and I want you to play it tonight with me. I have confidence in you."

Mother went straight home and washed her hair. She already had a simple and becoming white dress. She just tied her long black hair back and let it fall down her back, as she had no time for an elaborate upsweep styling. The young woman who dressed so modestly and played with such authority captivated the audience. The critics were all a-twitter at the debut of a formidable talent. Dad said that, despite the favourable reviews, the next morning at 9 o'clock Mother was in her place at the academy ready for her lesson.

Apparently Dad, born October 12, 1880, had no musical forbears of whom we know. There were teachers, clergymen, lawyers, physicians, sea-going types, poets, authors, but no composers. His sister, Mary Helen, five years his junior, told me that she could never remember when her brother wasn't composing either on the family's piano or on the organ over at the Anglo-Catholic – i.e., very high – St George's Church, Beckenham, in Kent. A Willan clergyman had been a staunch adherent of the Anglo-Catholic Movement at Oxford in 1833, and my grandparents were supporters. In the nineteenth century, two camps – 'high' and 'low' – within the Church of England disagreed intensely about the place of ritual and tradition in worship, just as today other issues threaten to tear apart the worldwide communion.

An early memory of Dad's that he shared with me was of setting off for church. Grandmother led the way with a lantern that could serve as a weapon, he followed close behind her, with Grandfather, close behind him, brandishing his shillelagh. Meg, the St Bernard, had to stay at home. She always knew when she wasn't going out with the family, for Grandmother was carrying her prayer book. At other times, Meg was Healey's guardian and later Mary's.

Mary became so proficient at ballet that a troupe under Anna Pavlova invited her to tour with it around the British Isles. When the company was to go to Paris, Grandfather put both feet down.

Mary had to resign, and that was that, she told me. People in England treated dancers as professional performers, but in Paris, or so her father understood, ballerinas were playthings for politicians and playboys. No daughter of his was going to be a dancer in Paris.

One of Aunt Mary's school friends became a lady-in-waiting to Princess Beatrice (1857–1944), ninth and youngest child of Queen Victoria and wife of Prince Henry of Battenberg (1858–1896); during the Great War, the family anglicized the name to 'Mountbatten.' Mary's young friend, of good family and connections but limited means, needed appropriate clothes for public occasions. A couple of plain, well-cut ensembles were fine, but hats were another matter. The two women would often spend hours together redecorating one enormous, brimmed hat with a selection of ribbons, flowers, feathers, stuffed birds, and pieces of silk in various disguises and suitable for a range of seasons and events. Aunt Mary recalled that she loved the challenge of rearranging and disguising the furbelows into new concoctions.

After Grandfather's death in 1913, Aunt Mary remained with her mother, caring for her as her blindness worsened until her death in 1938. When I visited my aunt after my father's death at 87 in 1968, she was well into her eighties and frail. I suggested to her that we take a 'Woodland Glade Excursion' – a bus trip for seniors through a forest, followed by a cream tea. She perked up instantly. Once on the bus, replete with older people chatting away, Aunt Mary told me how she had once flatly disobeyed her mother. It was the only time she had done so, but she had never regretted it.

It was October 1914. She was 29, and her mother forbade her to take a train, at night, from Brighton up to Victoria Station in London. She wanted to go because of her beau, an eligible suitor. The whole bus fell silent. Aunt Mary's voice was not harsh, but it had a carrying quality. His name, she went on, was Frank Churchwarden, and they had been dear friends for some time, with hopes of settling down together eventually. At the outbreak of war in August, Frank joined up. My aunt recalled his sterling qualities – her hero for sure

– his manliness, his sense of humour. "I couldn't imagine being married to a man without a sense of humour, although I have never been married at all," she wound up sadly. "I hope your husband has a sense of humour." Now she had the other passengers in her thrall.

"Frank's regiment was one of the first to be called to the front, and they were setting off for France from Victoria Station at 11 o'clock at night. I did so want to see him off. Mother was adamant about my not travelling like that by myself, but I have always been glad that we said goodbye." The silence on the bus was so profound that it seemed as though everyone was reliving memories of that terrible war. Frank was killed in one of the earliest offensives.

My grandfather James Burton Willan and his brother Thomas started out to study medicine. The family seems to have experienced a sudden reversal of fortune. Thomas's godmother made it possible for him to continue his education, but James Burton, though near graduation, had to drop out. He took a job in a chemist's shop in London. The only family member not appalled was his cousin and fiancée, Ellen Healey. They married, and the others turned their backs on a relative 'in trade.' Grandfather always remained somewhat bitter about the snobbish treatment, or so Mother told me.

In the months before the coronation of Queen Elizabeth II in June 1953, my father received an imposing gold-edged invitation to send in family names and dates for the special commemorative version of Burke's *Chronicle of the Landed Gentry*, enclosing a cheque for "collateral issue." Dad was furious. "If they are so anxious to have their records complete, let them do their own handiwork, and as for paying them to be included … " He was half-way upstairs, and I didn't hear the rest, which was probably just as well. When family members in England heard that the archbishop of Canterbury commissioned cousin Healey to write a homage anthem for the coronation, they suddenly remembered that they had 'colonial cousins.'

Dad's cousin William Willan became an architect. While still a student, he won a competition to design a bishop's seat in Canterbury Cathedral. It's still there, white oak, not overly decorated, and bearing a little plaque about its designer. He also restored the manor house at Chilham in Kent for a friend who so much liked the result that he asked Uncle Bill to restore the entire village as well as the church. When advertisements appeared in *Country Life* for 'genuine' fourteenth-century stone dwellings in Chilham, the family roared with laughter, or so Dad's cousin Angela Willan told me. Uncle Bill also restored parts of King's College in Canterbury so skilfully that now experts cannot tell what is medieval and what is his handiwork.

Aunt Mary thought him scandalous because he was a buddy of the 'red' dean of Canterbury and, according to her, polished off a whole bottle of brandy every day. I think that she exaggerated; he certainly didn't look like an alcoholic to me when I met him. My dear aunt used to meet a retired venerable archdeacon every week, and together they went over the horse-racing forms while killing a bottle of sherry. When their little 'flutters' came in, they celebrated with more sherry.

In the late 1880s, in Eastbourne, Dad left the family home for the Choir School at St Saviour's Church, where he received a fine musical education, but Oxford and Cambridge were financially out of reach. In London he became organist of various churches and a student of Dr William Stevenson Hoyt's, meeting two of Hoyt's other students: Gustav Holst and Leopold Stokowski. He also proof-read music manuscripts for Novello & Co. A thank-you note arrived for him one day from Edward Elgar for catching what turned out to be a slip of the pen, a sharp instead of a flat. Dad had a number of his songs published, and he was beginning to make a name in the musical world. Probably about this time he realized that he could never achieve his real ambition, to become a cathedral organist, for which one needed a degree from Oxford or Cambridge.

He qualified as a fellow of the Royal College of Organists at 16, the youngest on record. He originally took the exams when he was only 15, and the examiner had asked him if he were waiting for his father. He failed because the pedals were slippery and his shoes skidded about. The next time he tried, he rubbed chalk on the soles of his shoes and left a white trail on the carpet. But he passed.

Dad and Mother met by bumping into each other, literally. Winnifred Hicks-Lyne – 'Auntiewinnie' to us – a recital soloist and the toast of London, had later coached the greats, whose loving tributes covered the lid of her grand piano. She herself had been in the process of becoming a soprano of renown, a diva, and introduced some of Dad's songs at Wigmore Hall in London. In the midst of telling me about her halcyon days, and in her still-commanding voice, Auntiewinnie suddenly broke off. "Lovely sapphires, dear," she said, and continued right along. It usually takes a jeweller with a loupe to recognize the green stones in my ring as sapphires!

As Auntiewinnie recalled, she was apparently in a hall of the Royal Academy one day when Dad had some errand at the academy and accidentally brushed into the beautiful student Nell.

"It was chemistry," she said. "Absolutely electric."

The pair carried on what then constituted a whirlwind romance. Grandfather Hall had high hopes for Mother as a professional musician, and Dad was a young church organist, a composer with no university degree – promise perhaps, but not suitable for his daughter. Healey and Nell eloped in 1905.

Although they had played together in public before their marriage, Dad showed his Victorian upbringing by not wanting Mother to perform in public after their marriage. Years later, whenever Dame Myra Hess came to Toronto, she and Mother would get together and talk shop. Sometimes Mother dragged me along, and I had to endure Dame Myra's formidable stare, which seemed to say, "Nell gave up a career of certain fame to raise this object." The Chelsea buns of hair that she wore over both ears were as alarming as her intense gaze.

By 1913, Nell and Healey had become a family of five with my three brothers who entered the world in February of 1907, 1909, and 1911. They were proper little English lads of impeccable manners; Michael was now 6; Bernard, or Bunny, 4; and Patrick, 2. A number of Dad's works had appeared in print, and he had started several more – a few bars or, for larger works, a couple of pages. He had done some orchestral conducting, but cathedral organist seemed an impossible dream. His father had died the same year, and Grandmother and Mary settled together in Bexhill, not far from Brighton, an inconvenient journey for Dad. My parents were living in St Albans, with Dad commuting south into London, which they regarded as a temporary arrangement until they could afford London.

My memory of my grandmother Willan is of a slender woman with a soft voice who was nearly blind and possessed a wicked sense of humour. Dad told us that on one occasion when he went to see her because she was ill in bed, they sat and chatted. When he asked what she would like to do that evening, she sat up and said, "Let's go out and fight a policeman." You never knew what Grandmother was going to come out with. She was a very popular guest at Petworth Castle, which J.M.W. Turner made so famous; the family certainly was not as affluent as other guests, but apparently she was so much fun that people asked her everywhere.

In 1912, Dr Augustus Vogt, principal of the Toronto Conservatory of Music, visited London on an interviewing spree, searching for a new head of the Theory Department at the conservatory. Apparently seeing the growing number of Dad's compositions plus favourable reviews in London papers, Vogt sought him out and offered him the position. I think that Dad, 32 and with a wife and family, and even despite his successes as a composer, realized that the lack of an Oxbridge degree barred him from a cathedral position. So Canada it was – a bit off the beaten track perhaps, but a track with perhaps more opportunity.

As Mother recalled, Dr Vogt came to their flat to finalize the contract. Over tea, he mentioned that he was hoping to find two suitable staff members for piano and voice. Mother perked up. Moving to the edge of beyond was not her idea of bliss, but as a gold medallist of the Royal Academy she thought she might perhaps speak with some knowledge. Dalton Baker for voice and Viggo Kihl for piano, she suggested. Quite apart from their suitability, spouses Bess Baker and Ellen Kihl were two of her chums – if she really had to leave London, she wanted pals going with her. Viggo Kihl, with his wonderful Danish accent, had already made a reputation as a recitalist and soloist with various well-known orchestras. Dalton Baker had a distinguished career as a boy soprano. He performed for Queen Victoria, who loved music. She clasped him to her bosom and seated him on the imperial lap – an occasion that he was always happy to relate.

Dr Vogt took notice. Mother felt relief when she heard that Ellen and Bess would be heading to Toronto too. Dad arrived in 1913 in time for the autumn season. Dalton and Viggo travelled as soon as their schedules permitted. Mother followed in the spring of 1914 with the three little boys.

The city of Toronto in 1913 must have been a doleful, dour place in many ways, comatose and smug, on the outside anyway. It was certainly producing money, but outward signs of enjoying it were not seemly. Into this strait-laced milieu stepped my father, a typical young Londoner – urbane, witty, with an ever-present twinkle in his eye and never at a loss for telling a good story, sometimes ribald. He must have been a shock to Toronto, and I gather that 'Toronto the Good' was definitely a shock to him.

Nicholas Goldschmidt arrived in Toronto in the mid-1940s; on his first day, a Sunday, he recalled, he found no newspapers with his breakfast, no beer or wine with lunch, and no movies to pass the afternoon. "Vat sort of place have I come to?" he asked himself in that inimitable accent

In 1913 Dad arrived alone in Toronto. He soon started teaching at the conservatory, which was then at College Street and University Avenue, and as organist-choirmaster at St Paul's Anglican Church on Bloor Street East. Able to explore his new surroundings on his own, he found Toronto even more puritanical and a bit on the bigoted side. Employees at Timothy Eaton's department store downtown drew the draperies on the windows tight shut at closing time on Saturday and opened them again on Monday morning, thereby discouraging thoughts of worldly acquisitions and encouraging piety on the Lord's Day. Certainly a couple of notices in shop windows, such as "Help Wanted. No English Need Apply," my father found disconcerting and saddening.

Fortunately he discovered the Arts and Letters Club and kindred merry spirits. Without the club, Dad would most probably have cabled Mother to stop packing and to expect him home as soon as he could obtain a berth on anything travelling east across the Atlantic. Fortunately he was soon busier than ever, writing as usual for English music publishers and over the years adding several U.S. and Canadian houses to the list – in all just over 30, some sort of record, so Giles Bryant told me.

Mother and the brothers – Michael, Bernard, and Patrick – sailed for Canada in the spring of 1914. It must have been quite an experience for my mother. At that time, little boys and girls, at least in England, wore leather gaiters – miserable things with a hundred little shoe buttons reaching only to the middle of the knees. Apparently on board ship she would get the shoe buttons done up on six small legs and shoo the bodies out on deck, where there would be wailing and skirmishes, sometimes with tears and moans about how cold it was. So she had to reverse the whole operation. "In and out, in and out," she told me; "it was like puppies that couldn't make up their minds." Except that puppies don't wear gaiters.

The foursome reached Toronto in late spring, a couple of months before the Great War started, and the family moved into an apartment on Jarvis Street, then a 'good' address. Auntiewinnie's family, the Hicks-Lynes, lived there already, so that may have influenced my parents. Auntiewinnie told me that she and her family were visiting one day when Mother told the three rambunctious young Willans that their noisy play was disturbing their father, who was writing some music. It was important that they not disturb him, she added; his writing music, she explained in her soft voice, provided for them a comfortable home and good food to eat. Auntiewinnie commented, "They kept on playing, but in absolute silence." By September 1914, they were attending Coverley House in Havergal College down the street, a girl's school that accepted boys in the first grades. The family acquired a puppy, a foundling from the Humane Society, and called him Pete; he was of uncertain lineage but well above average intelligence.

The first summers in Canada the family spent at a cottage on Lake Simcoe, an easy ride on the radial electric railway from downtown Toronto. Dad's cousin Winnifred Willan from Victoria joined them. Professor Saint Elme de Champ of the French Department at University College, University of Toronto, was staying nearby, and he and Dad apparently hit it off. Papa de Champ, as we called him, had already married, but Madame de Champ could not bring herself to leave Paris. He and Cousin Win passed a very pleasant summer together. She never married. How many rules of conduct there must have been in those days, and crossing them could bring dire penalty – social ostracism, even loss of employment.

As the boys grew, and Pete along with them, the apartment on Jarvis Street became rather confining. Dad bought a house at 26 Park Road, convenient to Crescent School for boys. It was also near St Paul's Anglican, where he had been organist and choir director since 1913. It was 'low' Anglican, unlike the high churches of his upbringing. Mother, who had grown up in the low-church tradition, was happy about it. The boys went to Sunday School there, where, they told me, they learned to shoot craps and acquired a whole new vocabulary when the teacher was out of the room.

Late in 1919, Mother sprang her news: another Willan was on the way. Another move seemed inevitable.

PART I

The 1920s

CHAPTER TWO

And Then We Were Six

(1920–1925)

In 1920, the year in which my father became vice-principal of the Toronto Conservatory of Music and switched from St Paul's Church to St Mary Magdalene's, where he stayed for life, the family found a new home and I arrived on the scene. The move from 26 Park Road was somehow receiving one postponement after another. In those times it was not seemly, or so Mother thought, for pregnant women to appear in public without an escort. Dad was busy: springtime meant examinations to set and papers to mark; May and June brought fashionable weddings at St Paul's that required his participation, as well as graduation ceremonies in Convocation Hall at the University of Toronto. To cap it all off, housing was in short supply. Veterans returning from France in 1919 had made a significant dent in the housing market.

In early July 1920, I made it abundantly clear that if the Willans were to move before I showed up time was of the essence. They had better put their house in order, so to speak. After five hot summers in downtown Toronto, Mother believed that air would be cooler and healthier above the hill that ran close to St Clair Avenue. The problem was that houses were even harder to find in that area, which still had open fields. Suddenly Mother's trip to the hospital was imminent. She went to the Private Patient's Pavilion at the Toronto General Hospital, directly across from the conservatory.

Dad was frantic. He called into action Evelyn Pamphilon and Marion Jones, teachers at the conservatory and friends of both my parents. They found an old farmhouse in Moore Park – one of the earliest brick buildings on Inglewood Drive, overlooking the ravine. Dad snapped it up, more or less sight unseen. He figured, I suppose, that two women would understand what would appeal to another woman and would comprehend the family's needs.

I arrived on July 11. Soon out of the hospital with me in her arms, Mother was eager to see her new home. The taxi turned right off St Clair and made its way south on Inglewood Drive. It passed the imposing white-stone Mercer mansion (later briefly the residence of Gina Lollobrigida), the grand old Butler home in Queen Anne vernacular, the Rolphs' attractive place on the ravine, and two other dignified centre-hall homes. Then the taxi came to a stop in front of the most unprepossessing, narrow, three-storey, red-brick farmhouse, of no discernible architectural ancestry. Its saving grace for Mother was that it was above the hill – 10 points for location, 0 for charm. It must have been a shock to her. If some real estate salesman had whispered, "Location, location, location," Mother would surely have given him or her that frigid look that meant: "I have no comment."

She had just endured another shock – a custom of her strange new land. She had given birth to all my brothers in the comfortable and familiar surroundings of home, with a midwife in attendance, the English tradition. In Canada she headed off to a hospital that had a serious nursing shortage, the result of war's end and a baby boom. Nurses carried newborns three at a time to their mothers down a long hall. Mother told me that she felt alienated from her baby; waiting for the nurse to bring me – sometimes not up to her squeaky-clean standards – was distressing.

After Mother produced me, she remained with me in the hospital longer than the usual recovery. One afternoon, so she told me, Dad encountered Canon H.J. Cody, rector of St Paul's and later president and then chancellor of the University of Toronto, on College Street near the hospital. They exchanged pleasantries, and Dad told Canon Cody that he was on his way to visit my mother. "Then I'll go with you," came the reply.

The ensuing conversation in Mother's room centred on a trip to Europe from which the canon had just returned, where he attended a seminar in Vienna apparently on heredity. He was most enthusiastic about what he had learned, including the fact that if both parents had dark hair and dark eyes, the offspring would inevitably have the same. At that point a nurse brought in me, with fair, rather reddish hair and green eyes. There was a sudden silence. Mother was furious and declared that those savants needed to do more research. What's more, her first baby, my brother Michael, had exactly the same colouring. Canon Cody dropped the subject at once.

At the same Vienna gathering, papers and discussions had dealt with the latest treatments for cancer. Canon Cody told my parents that the presence of Canadians surprised the other participants; it seemed that the most important current work was that of Dr Hendricks, Mother's obstetrician, who had studied at McGill and taken postgraduate training in Philadelphia. Dr and Mrs Hendricks were our family's neighbours and friends. Mother had understood from Mrs Hendricks that her husband felt uncomfortable at the medical faculty – the result, it seemed, of prejudice from other faculty members and graduate students about a 'foreigner' from McGill invading them.

Perhaps because Mother had few really intimate friends, she very early took me into her confidence about matters that I did not understand at the time. With no morning-after pill or any known way to prevent pregnancy, even Dr Marie Stopes's suggestions were not fool-proof. Many women took matters into their own hands, a risky situation. The Willans had been a family of five when they left London, and that had seemed entirely sufficient to my parents.

To Mother's chagrin, she had become pregnant five years after they settled in Toronto. So she had taken matters into her own hands, and, I believe, not for the first time. On this occasion, however, she told me, she woke up on the bathroom floor in a puddle of blood and decided never to do such a dangerous thing again. So in the autumn of 1919, when she told Dad that she was pregnant and that she was not willing to risk her life another time, he was angry, she was upset, and they moved into separate bedrooms. She told me that she was tired of raising little boys and had made up her mind that this final baby would be a girl. I fulfilled her wish.

My parents had a deep and loving commitment, and sleeping solo – as they did for the rest of their lives – must have been extremely frustrating for both of them. They continued to adore each other at a distance – a situation that must seem completely foreign and very hard to imagine for young people today. It took me more than half a lifetime to realize the source of their occasional irritations with each other. Sometimes they wouldn't speak to each other for days. I don't think my father was unique in seeming to blame his wife for becoming pregnant – it just seemed to be an accepted attitude of the day. Pondering on such a situation brought a depth to my understanding when reading nineteenth-century novels, particularly French. Sometimes I felt guilty about what I seemed responsible for – breaking up a perfectly good marriage – but then there was nothing I could do about it.

Mother's godmother, a French lady who married into her family, was both a mentor and a friend to her. She taught Mother to cook, and Mother mixed French and English cuisine. Elaborate sauces were out – *'cuisine de touriste,'* she called it. So when she asked Mrs Vogt to be godmother to me, she hoped that I would have a similar friendly experience. Mrs Vogt lived only a few doors away on Inglewood Drive, but we hardly ever met. I suppose she felt that sending me a present each Christmas until confirmation at 13 fulfilled her obligation. The last gift was the best – *Pride and Prejudice* in blue Morocco leather, with gilt-edged pages and a blue ribbon as bookmark. It gave me pleasure just to hold it then, and I still treasure it and its contents even as the bookmark withers with age.

Early in the concert season of 1920–21, Dad and Mother apparently went to Massey Hall to hear Leopold Stokowski conduct the Philadelphia Orchestra. It was Mother's first outing since my birth and difficult for her, I learned later. She was 38, which many people considered a bit risky for bearing a child. Dad and Stokowski had not seen each other since Dad had left England. In the intermission, he went down from the balcony to see his old friend and left Mother, who was still finding stairs 'a climb.'

"Where's Nell?" Uncle Leo asked my father. Dad told him that she was still recovering from childbirth and an extra trip down and up the stairs would be tiring for her. "Then I'll go and see her," and he bounded up to Mother's seat, to the astonishment of neighbouring patrons.

Conductors do not as a rule mingle with the audience midway through a performance. Mother later told me that Uncle Leo's wife had also just produced a daughter, and apparently the pair of them compared their offspring, bragging about relative sizes. They must have looked like a couple of fishermen trying to impress each other. "She is so nize," he kept saying about his, and Mother had her say about me. For years a doll used to arrive on or about my birthday from Uncle Leo.

I seem to remember finding it odd when I read many years later that Uncle Leo had married Gloria Vanderbilt, a fabulously wealthy young woman four years my junior. I wondered what the 'so nize' baby thought about it – a stepmother not quite her own age.

My father switched churches soon after my christening. When he had arrived in Toronto in 1913 and became organist and choirmaster at St Paul's Anglican on Bloor Street East, it was the largest church in Canada then and it possibly still is. It catered to Rosedale and Bay Street Anglicans, probably the wealthiest congregation in Toronto or in Canada. Mrs Cody, the rector's wife, had strong views on the music and especially on the hymns for Sunday services. This rather constrained Dad's choices, with which he sought to complement readings and the service in general. He put up with her suggestions, but he had a mark in mind beyond which he would walk out. One day she overstepped the mark. It was a few months after my christening in the church in 1920, and he simply resigned.

He knew that a high Anglican church was looking for an organist and precentor, and that knowledge may well have sparked his decision. He called up Father Hiscocks, the rector at St Mary Magdalene's, at the corner of Ulster Street and Manning Avenue, and told him that he knew of an ideal candidate. Father Hiscocks invited him to bring the person for dinner. Dad, of course, arrived alone. The rector opened the door at Dad's knock and asked, "Where's the candidate?" "Won't I do?" came the reply.

The two men decided everything over dinner, and Dad served as organist and precentor there until his death 47 years later. His salary would be a lot lower at the smaller and poorer church, but Mother just shook her head. The new place suited him better, and that was that. His pay became even less during the Depression, when St Mary's, despite its prestige in the world of religious music, nearly locked its doors, unable to afford heat. Dad told Mother after an annual general meeting in 1931 or 1932 that he had volunteered to take a 50-per-cent cut in his meagre salary. Again she just shook her head. When I said, "Oh dear," at her news, she told me that when you marry a composer of genius you just have to accept the reality that music is more important than anything else and that we would manage somehow.

At St Mary's, Dad could develop his own interests in Gregorian plainchant, at which he became an authority. Father (later Monsignor) Ronan used to call him regularly for help and information on the subject until he too became a leading expert in the Catholic church. How they would have chuckled when Gregorian plainchant topped the charts for a while some fifty and more years thence.

Its moving from esoteric and arcane to the hit parade would have seemed incredible to them both.

My first memory dates from a couple of years after we moved into 139 Inglewood. I was in my wicker pram, an elegant affair with a creamy pale-green silk lining and a creamy silken fringe on the hood. How I hated that fringe: it swayed to and fro like a windshield wiper on an automobile, obscured my view, and made me dizzy. It has given me a lifelong dislike for any and all fringes and things that sway.

Anyway, we – Helen, who looked after me, and I – were crossing the St Clair Avenue bridge, with its wooden planks, which made a pleasant, rhythmic sound when horse-drawn delivery carts and the odd car rumbled over it. The sidewalks were wooden planks too of course, and my carriage was making its own gentle rumble. The bridge's wrought-iron rosettes and railings appealed to the dogs, who could lean out from behind them and watch for squirrels. The yelps of excitement must have confused the squirrels, coming at them from treetops.

Suddenly swaying and looming towards us was a white building!

Despite the fringes, I sat up and gaped. Horses were drawing a building the size of a house on some kind of platform, and somehow I knew that it was part of a church – perhaps a steeple or a cross gave it away. It approached very slowly, coming right at us. The planks of the bridge were groaning or growling – who knew which? – under the weight. It was a most disturbing sight. What on earth could be going on? I wondered.

"It's only Christ Church, Deer Park," Mother told me when Helen had pushed me home. "They are going to build a bigger church of stone," and she added, "and Miss Loring and Miss Wyle have bought the old one for their studio." This moving structure was probably the original wooden Christ Church, Deer Park, which Grace Church On-the-Hill at Lonsdale and Russell Hill had used since about 1910. Christ Church had rebuilt in brick in 1910 and was now reconstructing in stone; Grace Church was putting up a larger parish hall to replace the former Christ Church, which it had turned in 1911 into a parish hall after it proved too small as a place of worship. The wooden Christ Church was on rollers again, now on its way to Glenrose Avenue, according to Mother, one street north of us.

The Sunday School building from Christ Church, Deer Park, landed in 1910 at 110 Glenrose Avenue, just east of Clifton Road and of today's Mt Pleasant Road, according to some people, but the area then was still mostly fields. Miss Loring and Miss Wyle ('The Girls') acquired 110 in 1920; sculptors need large spaces: the board-and-batten structure was available, cheap, and perfect. The two together could just afford it: studio, sleeping quarters, a kitchen, everything they wanted. They soon became neighbours and good friends of ours.

Early in their tenure on Glenrose, the Church of St Mary Magdalene commissioned Miss Loring to create a rood – a large cross with the figure of Christ – to hang over the edge of the chancel. She hired a male model and told him to present himself at the studio on the appointed day. He showed up, and she instructed him to go to her bedroom and disrobe. She had left her handbag on her bureau with all their cash for the month's food for themselves and their dog and cats. She waited a reasonable time, and finally they both opened the door to find that model and cash had disappeared through an opened window. They were furious: no money, no model, and no means to hire another, and no time to lose if they were to receive payment for the work. So Miss Wyle disrobed, more or less, and became the model for Christ on the cross at St Mary's.

They were a lively pair, owners and lovers of dogs and nature and givers of great parties. One summer evening guests filled their studio, which became uncomfortably warm. Miss Loring, the large, motherly one, was wearing a sort of pyjama outfit, very 'Jazz Age' and quite sheer. She was the one who smoked a lot. Standing in her doorway, with cigarette in hand and the light behind her, she made a most interesting sight. Suddenly some neighbours – men who took their dogs out for an evening stroll, not arty types, not invited to the party – found it necessary to linger on the other side of the street. Miss Loring couldn't have cared less. My parents recalled the subject at breakfast next morning with great hilarity. It seemed to me that they both felt that the neighbourhood needed a little lightening up and that 'The Girls' were the ideal people to do it.

The pair bought a huge, old, black touring car – if not a Model T, something of similar vintage. They never pushed the top down that I remember, but they never wound the windows up either. Their dogs loved to hang out over the side, passing comments to other dogs and generally having a great time. Miss Loring drove the buggy like a demon up the Yonge Street hill. When other vehicles were faltering, having flat tires or whatever, she just sailed through the traffic like a tank, with their big shaggy black dog aboard, his tongue hanging out the side of his mouth. Whenever 'The Girls' and Mother converged on the grocery shop – an early version of Loblaws on Yonge Street – 'The Girls' always packed Mother, her bags, Pete (or later Nicky), and me, if I happened to be along, into the back seat with whichever dog they had at the time. Miss Loring had a great deep laugh, and Miss Wyle, tiny beside her, with a man's haircut à la Beatrice Lillie, smiled a lot.

Sometimes, I gathered, people who didn't know them as well as we did wondered if perhaps they had a sexual relationship. I don't think so. They always seemed to be good friends. Prior to their move and while they were still in their separate studios downtown, Miss Wyle's partner, also a sculptor, had a jealous wife. There was talk of footprints in a sculptor's inevitable plaster or marble dust. In those days divorce was difficult and messy. Miss Loring's beau was a German national, and in the midst of the war her father had taken charge and broken them up.

That annoying fringe on my pram featured in another early memory. Mother was pushing the carriage this time, wearing her billowy dark-green cape. I couldn't see it, but I knew that it was there, and I loved the dramatic way it swerved around her in any kind of breeze. She pushed the carriage to a dirt track that has since become Ridge Drive, on the edge of the hill. It overlooked the city a long way off. Suddenly we both spotted flames bursting and shooting into the sky. Smoke followed. It was a huge fire down below us, a terrifying sight.

St Andrew's College was going up in flames. The smoke thickened and billowed, and we couldn't see the city beyond. I wanted to know if all the boys were all right – not my brothers, who were by then at Upper Canada College, but the boys in the school on fire. Those flames were a mighty force, unforgettable. I don't think that there were any casualties. The whole campus is now a park on Schofield Road, and St Andrew's took itself north to Aurora.

My parents must have shown me off one day when I was about two to some woman with a pronounced English accent, who apparently cooed, "What a de-ah little baby with de-ah little hands and de-ah little feet." On bright, sunny mornings, Mother put me outside in the carriage, and I sat out on the porch with no one to talk to – a very boring situation. So I greeted every passerby with an announcement of who I was, complete with a fake English accent. When the powers that be caught on to what I was up to, they exiled me to the garden in the back. That's bureaucracy for you.

Charmless as 139 was on the outside, its construction was sturdy enough for the brothers. The attic could and did withstand the assaults of the three vigorous youngsters, who fought regularly and often. Bunny and Pat, who shared the large front room, eventually painted a white line down the middle of the floor as a territorial marker, just like a pair of wolf cubs might do. Michael held court in the back room, and the trunk room in between served as a buffer zone.

One sunny morning the brothers figured that it was time that I was up on my feet. They cleared the flowers off the dining-room table and lifted me up there. One of them went to push me from behind, one to beckon me from the other end, and one at the side to cheer me on, no hands allowed. There was no help for it – it was like having someone throw you into a swimming pool, sink or swim. It was walk or fall off the table. With a lot of arm swinging, tiny steps, and sheer terror, I managed to place one foot in front of the other and navigate the length of the table.

The brothers called for Mother. "She can walk," they shouted. They had to shout, for they were playing a record loudly on the gramophone, "Yes, We Have No Bananas"! Dad of course was down at the conservatory. They played another record at high volume when Dad was not home, something about blackbirds. When they shouted, Mother came at once, but it wasn't her baby walking that drew her attention. Her canary, overcome by the banana song and the shouting, had a heart attack and literally fell off his perch. My first big entrance – and upstaged by a canary.

Tea at four o'clock was a ritual in our home. Sometimes Ellen, Viggo Kihl's wife, joined us. She became very deaf, and Mother claimed that it was because her husband insisted that she sit up and listen to his practising long into the night. She told Mother that she had trained herself to sleep with her eyes open when she dozed, as she invariably did. The Kihls lived in a big old house on Beaumont Road, and she had their two sons to manage as well as their food, which seemed much more complicated than ours.

At dinner one evening Dad recounted to us a recipe of Viggo Kihl's, which he claimed was a Danish specialty. Dad would mimic his friend's Danish/English speech patterns, adding "you know," always with emphasis on the wrong syllable and his own pronunciation. Preparing the dish in question involved stuffing a goose with a chicken, I think, then stuffing that with a duck, then that with a quail, then a pheasant, and I think you finished the process with a lark. I may have left out one item of poultry or got the order wrong. It seems to me that there were more unfortunate birds in this mixup. Mother shook her head. "Ellen would never agree to that," was her verdict.

Ellen Kihl carried a cumbersome contraption in front of her into which she encouraged people to bellow. She held a trumpet-shaped device in her ear, but I suppose that she could turn it off when her husband thumped on the piano. She had a lovely sense of humour. The screens in their house apparently did not keep out mosquitoes. "The big ones push the little ones through," she claimed in her highly accented English, which made her tales as funny as her spouse's.

When they had grown up, both the Kihl boys took off for New York. One became an artist, and I heard that he worked during the Depression under the National Recovery Administration (NRA), painting a mural in New York's Grand Central Station.

After Viggo Kihl died in 1945, his widow was almost destitute. Mother tried everything that she could think of to see if Ellen were eligible for some sort of widow's pension. Whatever the rules were, she did have some success. On a hot afternoon in midsummer, Ellen Kihl, not a young woman, walked up the hill from Beaumont Road to Inglewood Drive bearing a special Danish queen's cake, which had many layers, each with a different creamy filling. It was her way of thanking Mother, who found the cake's grandeur embarrassing, as she did the likely cost of the ingredients.

Back in those days, residents of Moore Park seldom put their dogs on a lead when they walked them. Most canines behaved very well and just trotted along with their humans. Our old Pete simply asked to go out when the spirit moved him, and somebody simply stood up and opened the door for him. Sometimes, I think, he went calling on other dogs; seeing a couple of canines having a stroll by themselves was not an uncommon sight. They seemed to have their own social life, without chaperons and restrictions.

One day in 1924 Pete requested an 'out, please,' and I reached up as high as I could and turned the door handle. Shortly afterwards someone called the grownups outside. Pete had been run over and died at once, perhaps from a heart attack. It was all over with great suddenness. He had been losing his hearing, but nobody realized that he was too deaf to hear an approaching car, or maybe he was thinking about something else. But it was I who opened the door, and I carried a scar for many years.

Shortly after Pete's funeral and burial in the garden, with the brothers officiating, Dad was travelling on the Yonge streetcar before St Clair had a car of its own. The conductor asked Dad where Pete was, as he hadn't seen the dog lately. He was very sorry to hear about the death of the distinguished freeloader and told Dad that Pete's host of admirers would miss him very much. The question about the dog's whereabouts had surprised him, Dad told me years later. He had had no idea that the conductors all knew Pete by name.

The Yonge car in the early 1920s rode up and down Yonge from almost the waterfront to Heath Street, just north of St Clair. It turned around in the little park in front of Christ Church, Deer Park, opposite Yorkminster Baptist, again because attending service was so much a part of life; the streetcars followed the congregations as the city expanded. There was always transport for Sunday worshippers. The city developed the little park when it extended the carline all the way north to Eglinton Avenue and no longer needed the turnaround.

Dad had asked the conductor how he knew Pete. Apparently the Yonge car had a sort of cow catcher on the front, and good old Pete entertained himself by walking from our house over the bridge to Yonge, hopping onto the cow catcher, and riding it all the way downtown and back. He jumped off after the turnaround at Heath and trotted home. As Dad pointed out to me, don't whine about boredom – just follow Pete's example and find something interesting to do.

The English baritone and singer Dalton Baker had joined the staff of the conservatory in 1914, after Mother suggested him in London to Dr Vogt, and became soloist at St Peter's Catholic Church on Bathurst Street. One Sunday during the Great War, after morning service – he at St Peter's and Dad at St Paul's – the two met and walked together on their way to their Sunday dinners. Mr Baker was the sort of person who stated his opinions in a ringing English voice and intended his pronouncements to be the uttermost word of wisdom from the almighty. He had started off as a boy soprano – a celebrity – and it's always hard for such a person to become a normal teenager when the voice inevitably cracks. This Sunday, he opined in his usual way, à propos of nothing, that only a German could write a fugue like Rheinberger or Reger. Perhaps the organist at his church had sent worshippers on their way with a mighty Germanic postlude ringing in their ears.

Dad replied, "Oh, do you think so? We shall see about that." His friend's ex-cathedra pronouncement so riled him that he immediately set to work on something that would be on the grandest scale. The result was the *Introduction, Passacaglia and Fugue* (1916), a work of such towering majesty that Oxford University Press immediately published it. It is apparently extremely difficult to play. Dad's own copy had what Giles Bryant, the music historian and organist, calls a 'crib' in it, to make it easier to turn a page on the music desk when all ten fingers and both feet are very busy.

Giles also told me, when we were sorting out Dad's manuscripts after his death, that to play that work reasonably well is to an organist the equivalent of what the *Paganini Variations* is to a violinist. If you can carry it off, you have mastered your instrument. Dad frequently received requests to score the '*IPF*,' as he called it, for orchestra. But he wanted never to touch it again, just to play it. Knowing when to leave well enough alone, he told me, is the mark of one who knows his trade. His pupil and biographer, Fred Clarke, retired chair of Music at Queen's University, has since scored the *IPF* for orchestra. He did the same with Dad's sketches for his *Requiem* (c. 1914–18) and completed the work, another majestic score that Oxford University Press then published.

In the 1920s, Dalton Baker did acquire a motor car – typically for him, the most extraordinary automobile that we had ever seen. It looked a bit like a state carriage with a motor where the white horses should be. It had only one door on each side, so everyone had to climb up and over anyone else and manoeuvre into the back or the front. Crystal vases for flowers attached to each side contributed to the elegance. Upholstery in a soft shade of green covered the whole interior. Such opulence! I wonder if it had somehow strayed north from Hollywood.

On our first outing, with Dalton Baker driving, Bess in the passenger seat looked rather like Queen Mary in her turban. Mother, Dad, and I were in the middle back, and somehow Pat Baker shoehorned herself in. Her brother, Hugh, and my brothers had escaped this picnic. We had to stop a few times for Pat to climb over everybody and leap down to the side of the road. She seemed unable to keep her breakfast secure when the car was moving, and the problem was even more noticeable on the way home. Of course a grand alfresco banquet was no help to her.

In the custom of the day, we had a couple of flat tires too, but that was par for the course. Even in the 1930s, when my brothers and their friends thought of a drive to Buffalo as a big adventure, they bragged about the number of times that they had to reinflate the tires. Carrying a kit with red rubber bandaids and a bicycle pump was standard practice. Not long after the memorable picnic, the fancy model with the pale-green décor and the flower vases disappeared, and Dalton Baker started driving a black 'flivver' like everyone else.

Fish for dinner on Fridays was a command performance both in our home and at boarding school and for many traditional Christians. Hailing from a country where good seafood was readily available, Mother soon found an excellent source, and we ate fish at least twice a week. Many of Mother's ideas on nutrition were well ahead of her time. "If it swims, we have it," was the slogan of fishmonger Sid Perkins in the St Lawrence Market, her regular supplier, close to Union Station, where the seafood arrived. The fish would reach our front door in a van – horses drawing it eventually gave way to a chassis with a motor out front. The van was white, with a raised, glistening enamel fish with a great glassy eye on each side – an imposing sight. The neighbours patronized Mrs. Chambers Fish Market at Yonge and St Clair. Mother felt that Mr Perkins was closer to the source and hence that his stock would be fresher.

One afternoon probably in 1924, I was in the kitchen when Mr Perkins delivered a big fat fish. Mother had no help that afternoon and started preparing our dinner. I asked what she was doing, and she told me that she was scraping off the fish's scales, which weren't good to eat, and that it was something that every young woman had to know how to do when she married. I declared that in that case I should never marry. I asked Mother how old I was. "You are four, and you know that already. Now go upstairs and get into your Sunday frock."

Dad came home early. Mother changed her outfit as well, and the three of us set off for Massey Hall in a car from Deer Park Livery, Mother's favourite form of transportation for any important event. It was a twilight concert, something that Luigi von Kunits, conductor of the New, later Toronto Symphony, had invented the previous year. Probably the orchestra was playing something of Dad's, because we three sat in the front row of the first balcony. It was my first symphony concert. The concerts were at twilight or thereabouts because in the evening players worked in movie theatres before the 'talkies' came along.

The program I cannot recall, except that a singer, Miss Bacon, was the soloist. Miss Bacon's gown was of red satin; the colour matched her name, uncooked. Every time she took a deep breath, the shiny red satin rose up and down her front. I thought it both hilarious and unfortunate. At the dinner table that evening after the concert, Dad asked me what I thought of my first concert. I told him I thought it very funny that Miss Bacon wore a shiny dress the colour of her name that heaved up and down in the bright lights whenever she breathed. "I think we have an up-and-coming music critic in our midst," my father remarked. Oddly enough, I did become a music critic on the *Hamilton Spectator*.

Not long after the Bacon spectacle, Mother took my biggest, showiest hair ribbon and told me that I was lending it to my father. Oh. Yes, of course. What on earth could he want with it? "Wait and see," said Mother. "And as a thank you, you are coming to a concert in the conservatory Performance Hall." The members of the staff were apparently arranging some sort of benefit event for the students.

Sure enough, at one point in the proceedings, my father walked out on stage wearing a frilly yellow frock with my hair ribbon up on top of his head. I couldn't believe my eyes. He sat down at the piano pretending to be a very fidgety little girl doing her recital piece. One of the other teachers introduced him and told the audience that he/she would play a new piece, "The World Is Waiting for the Bunrise." Another staffer, a voice coach, also had dressed himself as a little girl and sang a falsetto rendition. I was the only person who did not howl with laughter. I must say that Dad put on a most dramatic performance. When he finished, the applause was thunderous.

Over many a year I was able to sort out what had happened that day. Dad's version of the episode was that Ernest Seitz, teacher of piano on the staff and well known as a soloist, had approached Dad one day long before I was born to ask him to arrange a melody that had occurred to him while he was shaving. Dad did so. It was a simple tune, Dad told me, and lent itself to a gentle poignancy. The words, by Gene Lockhart, repetitious and hopeful, appealed to the feelings prevalent in the public in the years after the Great War. Chappell first published it in 1918, it was very popular by 1923 or 1924, and by 1925 it had become a real hit.

Somebody else told me that at some time in 1930, after the stock market crash that brought the Great Depression, Dad encountered Ernie Seitz on Bloor Street. Ernie seemed very pleased with himself. He had just received his usual and regular royalty cheque from Chappell – in the four figures, I believe, an unheard-of sum, more than many hard-working souls earned in an entire year. Dad had just obtained his royalties from Oxford University Press for, I think, something under ten dollars. He congratulated his friend and suggested that they have a cup of coffee on his meagre payment. Ernie never acknowledged or thanked Dad for arranging "The World Is Waiting for the Sunrise." I rather think that the word circulated around the conservatory. Musicians are great ones for gossip, which may have inspired "Bunrise." Whenever any mention of the affair arose, Dad just shrugged. But when I first began to receive payment for my writing, he was insistent that I take care to protect my primary rights. One learns by experience, he told me.

Because Dad never drove, people seemed to enjoy picking him up to take him down to the conservatory or wherever, although I know he rather enjoyed the walk to the streetcar, especially after the St Clair route opened about 1925. Dad never purchased a car. Poor distance vision had disqualified him from volunteering for the South African, or Boer War. Perhaps he didn't want to face another rejection. He always wore glasses, but to see something tiny he would perch his glasses on top of his head and peer at it closely.

St Clair streetcar service began partly to accommodate Sunday worshippers at the Church of Our Lady of Perpetual Help at St Clair and Clifton Road. The car turned around on the other (east) side of Mt Pleasant, and the congregation could ride home after church. When Toronto above the hill had expanded sufficiently to justify streetcar service up Mt Pleasant, the old turn-around point became a little park, which the city named for the two neighbourhood sculptors, and two small busts of 'The Girls' still grace the space.

It seemed quite normal to the brothers and me that Dad was so seldom home at dinnertime; after all, musicians work at night. For my fifth birthday, however, he promised Mother to come home early as a special treat. She and I walked up Clifton Road to meet him at the new St Clair streetcar stop. We waited and waited. Finally family friends Mr and Mrs Duncan drove by and learned of our dilemma. Mr Duncan suggested that we all go and have an ice-cream cone. At breakfast next day, Dad made no mention of his absence, so I assumed that he had just forgotten. Something very important must have come up – that was Mother's explanation, but I didn't buy it.

Hansel and Gretel was a story that I knew from one of the exquisite books for children that used to arrive regularly from Mr Tyrrell's bookshop on the west side of Yonge Street, just north of Bloor. When Mother learned that Humperdinck's eponymous opera was going to be on, she decided to take along this four-year-old. It was all very exciting, just as I had imagined it would be, until the beginning of the second act. That's when angels appear to guard Hansel and Gretel sleeping in the forest. Two ladders appeared on either side of the stage, and angels started walking down the steps as though coming from the sky – very convincing staging.

Next morning I came stamping downstairs to breakfast in a foul mood.

"Whatever is the matter?" Mother asked.

"Why wasn't I told?" I growled.

"Told what, dear?"

"Those angels were no bigger than me. Why wasn't I told I could be an angel?" I had felt outrage. If the director had found me too big, too small, too fat, too skinny, or if he had enough blondes already, that would have been fine, but he had overlooked me without giving me a chance, and that was too much. Father looked at Mother. "We have another performer in the family, I'm afraid." He did remember that he had an eligible daughter later when St Mary Magdalene's was casting for the Christmas pageant or some Arts and Letters Club production needed a young female.

Mother and the brilliant theatrical producer Dora Mavor Moore had run into each other at the Toronto Heliconian Club in the early 1920s and instantly formed a deep and lasting rapport. After a run of *As You Like It*, instead of preparing a 'cast party' Mrs Moore and her adoring actors put on a spoof of the play in the club. Ray Purdy, I think, who became a radio personality on CFRB, was the duke, and there was a drunken revel in the Forest of Arden. The production needed a beastie to play up the inebriation. Fran Moore, the eldest son, was the rear end, and I the front, of a bear underneath a coon coat covering us both. Fran and I shared our theatre debut on the Heliconian Club stage when I was five, so he would have been eight. We made a great pair, harassing the other players underneath the picnic table and really sinking our teeth into the part. I was hooked.

CHAPTER THREE

Sea Change

(1926)

It was early 1926, one of those January days that we used to have, so cold that it was no fun for me when Mother bundled me up in heavy, bulky sweaters till I could not bend my arms. She would plunk me down to play in the back garden as immobile as a snowman and soon almost as frozen. Fresh air was obligatory, but it was not enjoyable. This particular morning I escaped the ordeal, and Pat was home from school. How curious.

Dr Oliphant came to call, which was also curious, since nobody was unwell. Both Pat and I were to receive our vaccinations. Pat had his on his arm. When the physician directed his scalpel at my arm, Mother protested, and I had to take down a stocking. Physicians gave vaccinations in those days by lacerating a skin surface and introducing dead smallpox virus directly into the cut. Dr Oliphant made light of the situation by scratching this way and that, telling me that he was drawing a Union Jack on my leg.

So that's how I figured out that Mother was going to take Pat and me to England. Ostensibly we were going to see 'Grannie,' Dad's mother, our only grandparent still living, but our parents had other ideas as well. The position of organist and choirmaster at Chester

Cathedral was open, and, as I later found out, there was interest on both sides.

In a great and glorious snowstorm, after waving goodbye – the neighbours called us 'the waving Willans of Inglewood' – we three and our trunks headed off on our adventure. A taxi took us to the grand North Toronto Railway Station on Yonge Street, well south of St Clair; the clock tower there evokes the *campanile* of St Mark's Basilica in Venice. These days the restored building sells wines and spirits.

Just as we were arriving, the taxi lunged over a chunk of snow or maybe ice, jolting Pat so hard that his head hit the vehicle's ceiling. I laughed because he did look funny bouncing up like a jack-in-the-box – not a clever move on my part. Mother had to stop a fight before she had even paid the driver and organized the luggage with a 'red cap' porter.

On the train for Montreal each of us had an armchair in a parlour car. These chairs were quite wonderful. They swivelled so that you could see out either side of the train or turn your back on another passenger. When it was time for a meal, you lunged your way to the dining car through other carriages and wobbling connecting passages that clanked and gave you a sweep of freezing-cold air. A starched white napkin that the steward ceremoniously unfolded and placed on your lap, flowers on the starched white tablecloth, and a handful of knives, forks, and spoons made it all very impressive. I couldn't read, so the menu was no help, but food arrived anyway.

Mother's sister, Aunt Edie Church, met us at Windsor Station, and we taxied up the hill to a townhouse on Metcalfe Street, which long since gave way to a Sheraton hotel and now an office building. Pat and I met our cousins Bill, Hannah, and Ben, and Uncle Gordon as well when he arrived home from his dealings with the stock market.

There was some excitement in the house. Aunt Edie's cleaning woman had just fled. Of African descent, she claimed that she had seen the bad-looking man walking without any sound up the stairs to the second floor. She said that it wasn't the first time, and she had had enough. She also claimed that she had 'second sight' and that the man wore "old-fashioned" dress. Aunt Edie's cat must have had second sight too. It shrieked and hid underneath the stairway whenever the cleaning lady said that she saw the apparition. Hannah dragged the cat out, and we fed it some cream in a saucer, but it was too upset to drink. I have wondered if anybody ever saw a man in "old-fashioned" dress trudging up a non-existent staircase when the place was a hotel.

We had but a short visit – just time for tea and to heave a few snowballs around in a small garden at the back of the house. The Churches accompanied us to the docks to see us off on the SS *Montrose,* heading for Southampton. As soon as we found our cabin, with lower berths for Mother and me and an upper for Pat, my brother and I went exploring. We came across a gym with a mechanical horse, quite a striking beast without a mane. Pat heaved me up for a ride and turned it on. At once this maniac of a creature broke into a canter! I hung on for dear life and have never yet fully been able to make a horse do what I want it to do. Payback for laughing at Pat's ascent in the taxi!

First night out of port was another treat. We went to the movies! True, it was only a few shorts, cartoons, black and white, no sound, but it was a first for me, and I was spellbound. My favourite featured Flip the Frog the Milkman, a juxtaposition of idiocies that made me laugh so hard that nobody would have heard the words or the music if movies had already had sound.

Sailing across the Grand Banks off Newfoundland in January is not quite luxury cruising, and I doubt if stabilizers existed then. One evening Mother went to bed before dinner and showed no interest in Pat's offer to bring her a snack from the dining saloon. I managed to tidy myself up for dinner, and he and I staggered off, clinging to railings every step of the way. We made a grand entrance down the majestic staircase to find olives dancing about on the coconut mat at the bottom of the steps. I sat down on the lowest step to watch their ballet, and we cheered them on, laughing at their hops. It was just the sort of sight about which Dad might have composed a limerick or written a little tune.

There were no other diners – how strange! Our steward put out more olives on our solitary table, and they took off, bouncing out of the dish and then heading straight for the coconut mat to join their fellows. I chased them around on the floor for a while until the steward brought us some food. It must have been especially to our liking because after the meal I wanted to tell Mother about it and about the olive dancers. But she just rolled over in her bunk and forbade me to mention food. Oh well, time for bed anyway, no movies tonight.

We stayed in London with Uncle Jack Hall, Mother's eldest brother, and in Bexhill-on-Sea along the south coast with Grannie and Aunt Mary. The two women would walk down to the sea most afternoons to buy shrimps, newly boiled and skinned right on the shrimp boats, for tea. They were fresh and tasted much better than shrimps from Sid "If it swims, we have it" Perkins. One morning at Bexhill I came downstairs a little late for breakfast, and Grannie's maid bade me "Good morning," but I knew that I was late and rushed past her. Grannie caught me and reprimanded me for not wishing Rose a good morning. I had to go and find her and apologize.

Pat soon found a stable whence he could ride out on the sands. Grannie approved. She wanted me to ride as well; it surprised her that I had not had lessons. I suffered through my initiation. My horse always knew who was boss, and after a couple of experiences Grannie released me, thank goodness.

When we were in London, Uncle Jack was busy most evenings as concertmaster of the Crystal Palace Symphony Orchestra. One day Mother took Pat and me to hear the orchestra in its colossal home, an astonishing experience. We walked down aisles of immense Egyptian columns, apparently the same size as the originals in Luxor. Greenery everywhere, even full-size trees that nearly reached the glass roof. It seemed a sort of fairyland covered in glass, and then the orchestra played a matinee concert.

Uncle Jack's house was in Upper Norwood, a section of London that gained a bit of a reputation. I overheard the grownups discussing the house a street or two over, which King Edward VII had almost bought for one of his lovely ladies. The deal fell through when the name of the secret buyer surfaced, and publicity was sure to follow.

You don't expect to see Niagara Falls in motion on a trip to Britain, but Mother and Pat wanted to visit the Empire Homes Exhibition at Wembley, a sort of world's fair. They dragged me along – apparently there was no one with whom they could leave me. Off we went to see the sights at Wembley. Mother bought me little wooden beads to amuse me, and I still have them. The exhibition was all as boring as could be to a five-year-old until we reached the Shredded Wheat booth, a replica of the familiar box, and, wonder of wonders, a machine that rolled over and over on itself making shredded wheat. So that's how they did it! I refused to budge, and the device so enthralled me that the man in the booth offered to take care of me for a while so that the others could see something more. Nothing could move me. Breakfast coming out of a machine like that was too good to leave. It was spellbinding to watch wheat kernels become long brown strings that folded up with a wonderful rhythm and emerged as this familiar airy, crisp cereal.

The exhibit also boasted a miniature Niagara Falls – a real waterfall! Pat's trophy, which he showed me later, was an enormous olive stone, which someone had hollowed out and intricately carved with some sort of magnifying mirror inside. When you turned it one way you could see the Houses of Parliament, and the other way was Tower Bridge.

One morning when I woke up in Uncle Jack's home, the whole world looked grey – no sunlight, just dark. I ran over to the window, and everything had disappeared, only grey outside the window. Just a London fog, I learned, from everybody's lighting up coal fires in every room and some sort of air inversion. It was eerie. You literally could not see the houses across the fairly narrow street, and the fog muffled even normal sounds of traffic. It was gloomy. My aunt and uncle seemed to think it all quite normal – that's just the way it was occasionally.

When Mother was away in Chester going about the real reason for our trip, Pat and cousin Leslie and I were alone in the house one afternoon. That was most unusual. We were sitting around a table in a room off the garden at the back of the house when we heard a strange noise in a sort of fruit cellar down some stairs. It wasn't a real cellar – most houses in England don't have anything underground. The boys, both about the same age, went over to the door leading to the stairs to see who could possibly be down there, a place with no other exit. They opened the door and turned on the light. I had to know what was going on and stood between them, holding onto a leg of each. A young man in a sort of sailor suit, a middy and wide trousers, stood at the bottom of the stairs looking up at us. So sad was his expression that I can never forget it. He wore a charming little round cap with a red pompom and just stood there without moving. The boys shrugged, turned off the light, closed the door, and went back to their game. They paid no attention to anything that I said about the sailor. They didn't seem to have seen him, but to me he was as clear as day.

Later that same year, when we were back home, there was a picture one evening on the front page of the *Toronto Daily Star* showing a warship in the city's harbour. The crew had lined up for the picture, and each of them wore a little round cap with a pompom. Since I still couldn't read, I asked Mother who they were. "Sailors from the French navy," she told me, "and they always wear that little hat." I tried to explain about the sailor in Uncle Jack's fruit cellar, but even she paid no attention and probably didn't believe me.

England in the winter and spring of 1926 was having a crisis that would eventually lead to a general strike. Workmen's wages had not gone up significantly if at all from pre-1914 levels. Prices had skyrocketed, and there was a sense of sullen anger in the people who did things for us. There was an elderly party in the Halls' house whom we called 'Aunt Sallie,' although she was not a relative of ours. It was one of her tasks to give me a bath every night. That woman surely had the intention of taking off a couple of layers of my skin. The bathwater was always colder than tepid, and there was little of it. She obviously was not crazy about her job.

As labour unrest grew, the government enlisted undergraduates from Oxford and Cambridge to drive trains and carry out other essential services. At a gathering of our relatives, one of our cousins at Oxford told us about his driving a train from somewhere north of London to Euston Station in the capital. Someone had shown him how to start it up, but nobody thought to tell him how to slow it down or stop it. The relatives almost died laughing during his description of would-be passengers on the platform at every whistle stop waving their umbrellas in frustration and rage as the train hurtled through. The cousin had become very afraid, although he didn't own up to it to us. The very last lever that he located brought the train to a graceful, dignified halt at the barriers at Euston. His listeners then described what might have happened if he had kept right on going down Gower Street in heavy London traffic! The stationmaster congratulated him for being the first driver to reach Euston right on schedule. When the cousin admitted that he hadn't made one single stop en route, they found him another job – quite boring, he reported.

One morning in London in early spring when we were at breakfast, a Canadian consular officer contacted Mother to tell her that we were to leave the country immediately because of the strike. So there we were, refugees from Blighty. We had to pack in minutes, say goodbye to Grannie and Aunt Mary by telephone, and report to Canada House, which put us on a char-à-banc – a bus with a retractable canvas roof. It was bitterly cold with the roof down, but the fear was that the strikers might figure that a khaki-covered bus travelling at high speed might be transporting soldiers. One of the passengers, a cheery sort, organized a sit-down gym session with everybody stamping feet and waving arms as the vehicle went hurtling towards Liverpool. We must have looked like a contingent from a local asylum going for a spree. It was quite a ride.

We stopped at midday in Oxford for lunch, which the officials had arranged for us. Pat nipped out and found a boot shop; Mother had promised him a pair of 'proper' English riding boots, and this was his last chance. He made it back to the restaurant, boots in hand, and somehow Mother, wanting to be fair to me, found a shop where she bought me a small tennis racquet. Even though we were fleeing for our safety, we were acquiring sports equipment to add to our bundles. Years later, when I came across the term 'non sequitur,' it seemed perfect to describe our Oxford shopping frenzy. I hadn't even known that I wanted a tennis racquet.

Flying along, half-frozen in that open-air bus, we approached the Mersey Tunnel. Our driver suddenly veered to the right, and we swung into the darkness, entering through the *exit* at full tilt. Most of us were hanging on for dear life. It all really alarmed Mother, who imagined us coming face to face with a big truck. Afterwards the driver claimed that he had some sort of intimation that a crew of strikers was ready to ambush us in the left tunnel.

It was long past my bedtime when we drew up at the Adelphi Hotel in Liverpool, and I was sound asleep. Somebody – perhaps a hotel employee, although most of them were on strike – slung me like a bag of coal over his shoulder, carried me upstairs and through a long hall, and dumped me on a bed. Many years later I stayed at the Adelphi, and the layout brought back so vividly my memories of that night.

Someone roused us early in the morning and handed us something to eat; then the bus took us to the docks. We then had what seemed to this small person a long walk to the ship through a narrow passage, as a guard of Royal Navy men stood at ease foot to foot. What on earth could they be hiding from us? I wondered. So, always curious to see what was going on and keen to find out what was on the other side of all those sailors, I slipped through the inverted V of one lad's feet to obtain a better view. There was nothing at all to see – no people, no guns, no dogs, no horses, nothing. On the other side of the walkway there was a real commotion. The Royal Navy picked me up by the collar and positively dumped me, rather rudely I thought, beside Mother.

When the general strike in England finally subsided, we had been back in Toronto a while. Apparently Chester was off our map. The funny thing was, before our trip, when Mother had spoken of 'home,' I had known that she always meant England. But as soon as we were aboard the SS *Montcalm* and out at sea, 'home' started signifying Canada to her. When we had returned to 139, the brothers, all born in England, were teasing me again, calling me a 'Canuck' as though that was some kind of inferior being or a rude word. I snapped back, "I am a Canadian and proud of it." They found other ways to tease me, but that Canuck label they dropped.

CHAPTER FOUR

Home and Hart House

(1926–1929)

There were still some strange customs in Canada that Mother never understood. The women on the teaching staff at the conservatory arranged a tea party and invited her as guest of honour. She arrived expecting someone to introduce her to everyone. To her utter amazement, her hosts seated her at one end of the tea table and expected her to sit there and pour out cups of tea all afternoon. This was an honour? In her experience in England, a maid in uniform poured tea, and another carried the milk and sugar around on a tray. Mother never figured that one out. She always had a cup of tea in the afternoon at four o'clock, either by herself or with a friend or maybe two. Bess Baker came frequently, and there was always a touch of formality.

Tea at the Bakers' home was equally formal. The guest kept her hat on. The ladies gossiped about musical personalities in town and reminisced about their days in London. This was in the era when children were 'seen but not heard.' The hostess served plain social tea cookies for my benefit and something that looked more interesting for herself and Mother. I used to stare at their cookies, willing them to jump onto my plate, but they were by invitation only. Pat Baker, home from school, greeted her mother but was too much older to ask me to play.

Mother's guests were often people who had come to Canada after the Great War to live in entirely different circumstances from what they had known in Europe. The Grand Duchess Olga was a charming lady, entertaining, a wonderful storyteller. She was a close relative of the late tsar and tsarina, Nicholas II and Alexandra, and had apparently been on holiday in the Crimea when the Bolsheviks detained other members of her family. Mother always made sure that tea that day was substantial, not lavish but filling, because she feared that the grand duchess could not afford to eat properly. One afternoon her guest brought Mother a present, an icon of the Virgin Mary, which she treasured.

Another guest was the Baroness Paumgraten, an Austrian refugee. I remember her as a jolly soul making light of her changed status. On one occasion she brought Mother some almond cookies and gave her the recipe for Mandelkakor. The ingredients are ½ pound of almonds, 3 egg whites, 1 cup of granulated sugar, ½ teaspoon of cinnamon, and 1 teaspoon of lemon rind. Wash but do not skin the almonds. Dry them in a moderate oven (350 degrees Fahrenheit) for 10–15 minutes. Put them through the food chopper. Beat the egg whites stiff. Fold in the almonds, sugar, cinnamon, and lemon rind. Drop the result by teaspoon onto a greased baking sheet. Bake in a 300-degree oven for 15 minutes. Cool and store in airtight container. The yield is about 40 small cookies.

All these ladies were trying to adjust to a new world, and they all had a deep appreciation and understanding of the arts in general, music in particular. Although Mother taught me to address them by their titles, she always reminded me that their titles were usually birthright or the product of marriage and that it made them no different from any other human being. It was a great lesson, just to accept people on their own, no matter how famous, or infamous for that matter.

After one of my many pleasant mornings playing with my friend Ann Lailey next door, I came home at lunchtime one day in 1926 to find Dad in a towering rage. This was most unusual. Something must have completely frustrated him, a man ordinarily so much at ease and saying funny things. Mother tried to be soothing. No effect.

Dad started up the stairs three at a time bellowing, "I HATE music." This was serious business to an impressionable youngster. Mother had brought us up to play quietly when Dad was home and composing or even just thinking about music. Her reasoning was clear and simple: Your father writes music. People pay him money for his compositions. He can't concentrate when you are making a noise. If he can't concentrate, then he won't write music. You won't have a nice house to live in and good-tasting things to eat. Period.

Dad was half-way up the stairs when I called out, very anxiously, "Daddy, you don't hate ALL music, do you?" Still in complete fury, he roared, "I HATE ALL music." I hadn't realized that grownups could feel so angry. I knew that I could when the brothers banded together to tease me. It now seemed as though the end of the world as I knew it was at hand.

I went next door to play with Ann. At some point in the afternoon her mother must have said something along the lines of how beautiful it must be to have your whole family loving music so much. So of course I had to put her straight on that one. "My father hates music," I told her solemnly. "In fact my father hates all music." Mrs Lailey dined out on that one. It took about three months for the precocious remark to reach Mother's ear. "You are never to mention what goes on inside the family to outsiders," said Mother in a voice that told me that she meant it.

One evening when Dad was home for dinner, he told us about a visit that he had that afternoon from a young woman who had some sort of musical ambition, probably to be a student. She must have dressed with great thought and care for the occasion, and she certainly made an impression on Dad. A vision in a dusty sort of pink with brown bits here and there, she wore a pink dress, a pink hat with a bit of brown, brown gloves and belt, and brown shoes with something pink.

The portrayal was entrancing, and I wanted to know everything. "What colour was her underwear, Daddy?" It was only a question to complete the picture, but the brothers and Mother and Dad just hooted. I learned early on that the best way to earn any recognition in that household was to make everyone laugh. So, for example, I would pick up a good-sized piece of watercress and announce: "tree in summer." Then I would bite off the leaves carefully, hold it up, and announce: "tree in winter." It didn't seem to be a bother for me to make them all laugh. Dad was my best audience, and I later heard that students, even Arts and Letters people, got some replays.

It was quite the usual thing for Dad to be somewhere else at dinnertime from Monday to Friday. The brothers dominated the conversation at the dinner table. Mother was keen to attend musical events, and, since Dad was not available and the brothers had their homework, I went with her to concerts and recitals. Whatever was going on in the arts community, Mother wanted to attend, and many mornings I arrived at school – once I started there! – too sleepy to take much interest in what was going on.

Ignacy Jan Paderewski hit a few wrong notes as I recall but played with such vigour for a very elderly man that nobody seemed to mind. Fritz Kreisler, the violinist whom everybody thought the most brilliant instrumentalist ever, played a few wrong notes too. Sergei Rachmaninoff, I remember, had such a grand and romantic touch, and the Australian Percy Grainger played as encores both of his party pieces, *Handel in the Strand* and *Country Gardens*. Once you heard Grainger play *Country Gardens*, it stayed in your head for a long time, irritatingly so.

As Friday night was choir practice in the church, Dad never went with Mother to openings at the Art Gallery of Toronto, so I accompanied her there. The gallery served tea and coffee at the openings in the central hall or atrium, Walker Court. An army of elderly women in black frocks, starched white aprons, and headbands with little black ribbons poured from the urns – no 'guests of honour' here. Central

Casting would give a fortune nowadays for those women and their look. Guests and assistants all knew and greeted each other – a most pleasant way to spend Friday evening.

Mother and I were regulars at the ballet as well. Boris Volkoff, a Russian émigré, produced a small and classically trained ensemble long before the National Ballet of Canada. His most talented pupil, Melissa Hayden, went to New York and became one of George Balanchine's most celebrated young ballerinas.

Hart House became part of my life in the mid-1920s, probably thanks to my father. The magnificent student centre at the University of Toronto opened on Armistice Day 1919, and Dad soon began composing music for Roy Mitchell and its splendid new theatre. Mitchell had begun to make a name in theatrical productions in England, and so it was natural for him to take part in the exciting first productions in Hart House. It was a lively scene. Vincent Massey, founder of Hart House and later the first Canadian-born governor general, and his brother, Raymond, progenitor of the theatrical Massey dynasty, were both active in the theatre. Members of the Group of Seven, including Vincent's good friend Lawren Harris, designed and painted scenery.

Roy Mitchell founded the Players Club in 1919 and asked Dad to compose music for his Hart House production of *The Chester Mysteries*. The manuscript is in the archives of the Music Library in the university's Faculty of Music. Dad completed it in a matter of hours – he subsequently told me that he worked on it overnight – and submitted it to Mitchell on December 19, 1919. The first performance took place three days later, and the theatre revived it at Christmastime for many years.

After the first rehearsal, Dad was walking home to Park Road through Queen's Park well after midnight. He was thinking entirely about the composition when a man accosted him; he thought the fellow ready for violence. He had only one arm free to defend himself, because the other was carrying the manuscript. A friend in

London with a black belt in karate had told him to strike upward with a blow to an assailant's chin, but he never thought that he would have to use the advice. He said that he instinctively swung out his right arm and caught the man on the chin with the palm of his hand. The would-be mugger fell on his back in the snow. There were no reports the next day of dead bodies in Queen's Park, so, Dad concluded, the thug must have survived.

My father loved writing instrumental music for plays; Mitchell's choice of repertoire really appealed to him, and he composed music for all ten of his Hart House plays. Those productions are a reminder that Toronto was not as culturally bereft as many people have assumed. Mitchell's efforts must have interested a wider audience, for he took off for New York in 1921 to become professor of dramatic arts at New York University. His friendship with Lawren Harris deepened when both took an interest in theosophy, and he published works on the subject in New York.

Dad and Roy Mitchell remained in close touch. Dad visited him in Brooklyn. The house struck him as singularly unprepossessing, but that across the street was most attractive. Both had been on the market when Mr Mitchell chose the ugly one. Dad asked him about his selection, and he responded that when he was inside his home he couldn't see its outside and he enjoyed looking at the pretty one across the street. I laughed at this story, but Dad smiled and shrugged, as if to say: it may seem an odd way to choose a home, but it pleased his friend, and that's what counts, so there we are.

Bertram Forsyth succeeded Roy Mitchell as director of the Players Club, and my father continued to compose for productions: *Pantaloon* by Sir James Barrie and *The Tempest* in 1922. He also wrote music for Forsyth's own play, *Castles in the Air*, produced first in December 1923.

In 1926 or 1927, when I had already attended Christmas productions, Mr Forsyth cast several youngsters, including me, in a show that was to run a week or two. The play was all about little girls and boys in a big town house befriending an equally juvenile chimney sweep. I was one of the privileged kids and received the part probably because of my father or through Mother's close friend Dora Mavor Moore.

After the first night, Nella Jefferis, the city's leading actress, produced a huge pail of Crisco and set it up on a stool in the middle of the dressing room. "Everybody dig your fists in and slather this stuff on your face and hands," she told us. It took handfuls of paper towels – there were no tissues then – to wipe off the goop, but the Crisco made it a quick and thorough job. Nella Jefferis told us that she used to wonder why her skin always seemed so much softer when she was in a play. One day it dawned on her that a daily slather, and two on Wednesdays and Saturdays because of matinees, were the best treatment that a face could receive. She figured that Crisco was probably the active ingredient in expensive and luxurious face creams. It worked like magic for the entire cast, especially for the poor chimney sweep, who had body paint from the top of his head to his socks.

Being backstage at Hart House was an education. We learned that one should never, ever leave the dressing room after the play with theatrical makeup still on. Doing so was unprofessional, period. One day, a young boy in the cast discovered the wind machine. One turned a handle, and the faster one turned it the greater the fury and power of the storm. We all became little storm troupers working up the sound of relentless, furious blizzards, until Mr Forsyth told us to knock it off. Blowing up a storm that way gives one a delicious sense of power over the elements.

Although the critics in the Toronto press wrote about the Players Club productions as though they were amateur theatricals, Nella Jefferis had had starring roles on Broadway before moving to Toronto. One role in 1917 had been in a play with Roy Mitchell in the cast, so perhaps he had a hand in her move to Toronto. She appeared in a number of productions in Toronto, sometimes in the annual spring show at the Arts and Letters Club – the hit of the town. She was a real star, although nobody recognized Toronto as a 'starring' community.

À propos of Canada and stardom: many decades later, Torontonian actor Donald Davis played in Samuel Beckett's one-character *Krapp's Last Tape* in New York. He told me that after the première on October 18, 1968, he had dropped into the opening-night celebration at Sardi's restaurant. Splendid reviews greeted him, and it suddenly hit him: he was actually starring in a hit on Broadway. He said that it was a great feeling.

He flew home to Toronto when *Tape* closed after a good run, and Customs and Immigration greeted him at the airport. "What were your reasons for being in the United States?" the officer asked him. His passport listed 'actor' as his occupation. "I am an actor," he replied. "Yes, but what do you do for a living?" the officer continued. Cultural life in Toronto changed during the twentieth century, but very slowly.

Throughout the 1920s, many a veteran of the Great War, missing an arm or a leg and with terrible memories haunting him, went from door to door selling things, and at 139 our supply of tea towels continually overflowed the kitchen drawer. One veteran in particular made our house a regular on his beat. His wife hemmed linen tea towels by hand, and he carried them about in a box that he slung around his neck. He needed both arms for his crutches. He never missed a sale at our home. Another former soldier with permanent injuries, but not serious enough to enter Lambert Lodge, sold Scottish toffee from door to door. He too became a regular, and when he was no longer up to it his young daughter took over his route, wearing her kilt. He could make the toffee, but walking through the streets was too much for him.

Perhaps Mother had her brother-in-law in mind when she simply could not turn down a veteran. Uncle Gordon Church had been a young lieutenant in the Canadian army. He led his platoon over the top of the trench in 1915 in the Second Battle of Ypres. A faceful of mustard gas partially paralysed him in a bent-over position. I overheard him replying to the brothers' questions one evening when he was in Toronto on business. They had shoved me out of the room, thinking the subject too gruesome for a little girl to hear about it. But I eavesdropped. He had been in agony as the medical people forced his legs straight in order for him to draw a breath. Too weak in the lungs for further active service, he became a staff officer under General Sir Arthur Currie after he could breathe sufficiently again, but his health was always precarious. He had only to cough or to sneeze and Aunt Edie would declare a red alert. Nobody could bring a germ anywhere near him.

Shortly after the war, when Uncle Gordon left the army and returned to Montreal, a lung infection hospitalized him. Since he was a stockbroker and couldn't work while in hospital, there was no money coming in. Aunt Edie tried writing stories for young boys – she had two sons of her own by this time. She sent her manuscripts off to English publications, *Boys Own* and *Chums*, which accepted every piece that she sent, but that could not provide enough income to support three children.

So she went to see Sir Arthur, pointing out to him that if one of his own staff officers had to go to the Salvation Army hospital, there must be many more officers and men in similar situations because of war injuries. She added that she thought the government remiss in forcing men who had fought and sustained such appalling injuries to depend on charity. Sir Arthur was instrumental in persuading Ottawa to acknowledge the country's indebtedness to servicemen who had insufficient injury to require permanent institutional care. Aunt Edie never knew if she had had any influence in the beginnings of the changes for injured veterans, but she and Mother certainly hoped so. Many businesses had held servicemen's jobs open for them, and one in Toronto welcomed each man back with a job and a gold watch as a token of thanks.

Before I could read, my parents decided that I should take piano lessons. They chose as my teacher Miss Olive Brush, one of Mother's friends at the Heliconian Club. Somehow she assumed that I could read, both music and English. We didn't really get along. I always asked Mother to play my pieces for me so that I had an idea of what I should produce. I practised on her massive square Beckstein, a beautiful instrument – Grandpapa's gift to her for her gold medals and sash at the Royal Academy of Music.

There was a recital coming up, and I knew that I had to memorize every note and play it well. My debut piece was that warhorse *The Merry Peasant*. I started it with my thumb on the note directly under B for Beckstein. I sorted that out and felt rather proud of myself, and so I stopped worrying. My Daddy and Mummy knew their stuff and just stood up in front of an audience, and so there was really nothing to it. However, the piano in the recital hall was a Mason & Risch. This blithe idiot started off, thumb under the M, even though it looked different. Oh well, never mind, just play, but there was something rather odd about this piano. But in the best professional tradition, the show goes on, no matter what. Even the black notes weren't lining up properly.

At the end of the performance everybody else's doting relatives were cooing at the lineup of little prodigies. I overheard a lady saying, "What odd pieces they give children nowadays." Mother was more direct: "What happened?" I tried to explain about the piano's shortcomings but didn't go far. I suppose that real musicians simply cannot conceive of such a defence.

Miss Brush, her sister, Teresa, and their father all lived together in a nice old house on Lowther Avenue. Rose bushes filled his front and back gardens. The scent as you walked past the house was delicious. He was so proud of his roses, and his garden was a showplace that had traffic slowing down to look and take a deep breath.

Our garden always had at least one white rose bush. Mother's forebears were from Yorkshire; hence her affection for the white rose of York. In London, Grandpapa had white roses also, apparently along with a fig tree that produced only one fig, which Aunt Edie picked off as a small child, much to his annoyance. I had no problem remembering which house was which when we reached the Wars of the Roses while studying English history – the white represented York. The Lancastrians were the 'bad guys,' but even so we had a few pinkish roses as well.

Our gardener was an interesting type. He told us that his father had been an admiral in the Royal Navy. He himself had grown up in a country house and had learned all sorts of gardening lore from the gardeners on the estate. I followed him around like a baby duck as he discussed which flowers were friends and mutually compatible and which should not be in the same bed. Mother figured that he was probably a 'remittance man,' of which Toronto had a few: some prominent English families would ship off to parts of the empire younger sons who probably wouldn't or couldn't amount to much in the professions. They provided these men with a regular subsistence allowance, on condition that they stay out of sight, out of mischief or at least limelight, and out of England.

The gardener was our furnace man all winter. Someone had to shovel coal into the furnace twice a day and remove ashes periodically. The brothers were too young for the job, and Dad wasn't going to have anything to do with it. I don't remember his ever being anywhere near the cellar; most English houses did not have cellars, and he did not intend to learn anything about what went on down there.

Coal arrived in a horse-drawn wagon or later, beginning in the early 1920s, in a truck. The deliveryman carried it from the curb usually up a driveway or a walk to a cellar window and dumped it into a coal bin. Then it needed transporting, shovelful by shovelful, across to the furnace. In the winter, our gardener/furnace man dropped by every morning before six and again in the late afternoon.

One day in 1927 or 1928 a couple of Armenians showed up at 139 Inglewood, selling a contraption to change a coal furnace into an oil burner. As our remittance man had occasionally overslept, Mother was curious about an automatic heating system that worked all night and kept the house warm first thing in the morning. She bought the device, and we became the first customer, the first home in the city apparently, to adopt the new invention. The Armenians worked away happily, replacing the coal bin with an oil tank as well as installing various bits of wizardry inside and outside the furnace.

The day of the official première arrived. The big old furnace was resplendent with a new coat of whitewash and was by now the size of an igloo for an extended family. Someone pulled a switch, the house shook, pictures skidded about on the walls, and we had oil heat. Dad named the furnace 'Boanerges' after an overly loud orator. Trust Dad! Many visitors nearly fell out of their chair at the sound of a locomotive taking off right underneath them, only to hear Dad's reassurance, "It's just Boanerges. Don't be alarmed." The creature lived up to its name and held court in its lair for over thirty years, until we retired it. A smaller, more feminine version replaced it, much quieter and half the size.

The remittance man did just gardening after Boanerges arrived and occasionally hung wallpaper and painted rooms. He knew a lot about how things should look, talked non-stop, and drove Mother frantic, but I loved to follow him about the house as well as the garden, probably slowing him down, but he never seemed to mind. Paint the ceilings lighter than the walls, he told me, so that the room doesn't seem to drop on your head. He planted pansies under Mother's roses, claiming that the two species needed one another in a nutritional way. He told me that the first flower that I knew by name, Sweet William, took its name from William, Duke of Cumberland, who led the English against the Pretender at the Battle of Culloden in 1746, with great losses to both sides in men and morale. Such a sweet scent, we agreed, to commemorate a massacre.

Disposing of the coal bin meant one less intruder to bark at for Nicky, our Humane Society dropout, whom some people said was a South Border Shetland sheep dog. He became a landmark in Moore Park. If he had been a human he would have run away to the circus, because entertaining us was his first priority. When he was just a tiny puppy – Pat's 1924 Christmas present from Dad, hence 'Nicholas' after the saint – he was minding his own business in our side garden where we kept the garbage bins. A foolish and thoughtless garbage man threw a big box over him, his idea of being funny, I suppose. That so startled poor little Nicky that he barked of course.

Thereafter he would bark at anyone approaching the house with a large container – a hod of coal, for instance. We had to explain to the innocent parties that the dog had had a traumatic experience and was not a biting sort, was not an attack specialist. It often took some convincing. Discussing Nicky's grievance with a garbage collector a few years after the initial experience was how we learned that our neighbours two doors down had been throwing out the *Encyclopedia Britannica* volume by volume over the previous few weeks. The people had thought that he wouldn't remove the entire collection all at once – too heavy for one load. He told me that he had saved the books and taken them into the cab of his truck to enjoy later at home. Did I know what had happened to volume 13? It seemed to be missing, and he was most unhappy not to have the whole set.

CHAPTER FIVE

Whitney, St Mildred's – and Mrs Moore!

(1927–1929)

At 139 Inglewood Drive, Mother and Dad were busy with matters musical, and the brothers with making their way through Upper Canada College. Our next-door neighbour Mrs Lailey informed Mother that it was compulsory to send a child to school by the age of five. So off I went one day in January 1927, six for some time now, to Whitney Public School. I hated it. I hated lining up with everyone out in the schoolyard and parading four at a time into our classrooms; meanwhile somebody pounded a piano with a popular tune about tiptoeing through the tulips as we stamped our feet in time. It felt like marching into prison, and until then I had lived a free spirit. It didn't help that the grade-one class was in the basement, which seemed cold and damp.

Everybody else had begun in September and had made friends. On my first day I had to stand up and say my name. Whether by inheritance from Dad or for some other reason, I had a slight stammer at times, and the two consonants I had trouble enunciating, especially when I was nervous, were M and W. The first day did not go well.

Fortunately incarceration at Whitney didn't last long. A number of us in that dank classroom caught scarlet fever, which was reaching epidemic proportions. Each of us went to the Toronto Isolation Hospital on St Matthew's Street, now a home for the elderly, I think, and renamed Riverdale Hospice. I arrived in the evening – before dinnertime at home and after dinner at the hospital. Being in a large room with hordes of other children, feeling hungry, lonely, and afraid, was not a happy experience. Much later that same night, another little girl came in with her mother, a nurse. Mrs Bland said that she would be glad to look after her daughter in a private room to relieve the stress on the nurses. The hospital could manage only two in a room, so Mrs Bland said that she would look after the sickest child along with her own.

The next morning life looked better for me. I had Muriel Bland to play with, and her mother was a very kind and capable nurse. Friends of my parents started sending in toys for me, so Muriel and I soon had a menagerie of stuffed animals and the sort of toys that supposedly develop the mind. It beat Whitney School by a long shot.

Many years later I met Miss Dove, who had long since retired as a teacher at Whitney and then married, and she told me that Dad had stormed into the principal's office demanding to inspect the grade-one premises, which he had learned were below ground level. After assuring himself that my version of going to school in a cellar was all too true, he sounded off about conditions harmful to children's health. Miss Dove told me that the class moved forthwith, to her relief, as she had complained more than once, with no result. I was no longer a student there: "He was just angry about bad conditions for all the children." I had had absolutely no idea that he had ever been inside that school or that he knew about our classroom, but his behaviour did not surprise me. Injustice generally riled him.

When Muriel and I finally received our discharge from hospital, we had to surrender the whole zoo for incineration. That's how seriously people took scarlet fever early in the twentieth century. Fortunately, I was able to tuck a couple of special treasures into the pocket of my dressing gown, and they escaped immolation. The hospital fumigated the gown, but nobody thought to shake out the pockets.

Medical procedures for the young seem to go in fashions. Still in the 1920s, paediatricians thought that slicing off youngsters' tonsils would prevent head colds – at least I think that's what they had in mind. While they were at it, they figured they might as well chop off the adenoids as well. The Doctors Hospital on Cumberland Avenue was my parents' choice for me. The procedure was painful, but it had its rewards. Because it made throats so sore and because swelling made swallowing a genuine pain in the neck, the victims feasted on ice cream for at least three days, which made the whole business worthwhile.

Even after a few weeks in the Isolation Hospital, I still had to stay in bed for weeks – no more Whitney for the rest of the school year! In the dense cold of those winters, Mother decreed that my window should stay closed at night and the door remain open for circulation. Mother was very big on air circulation, a habit that I still have.

So very early one morning all I had to play with was some small stuffed thing that I found in my dressing-gown pocket, a fellow escapee from the Isolation Hospital. I could hear someone coming down the stairs from the attic. I sat up at once, thinking that it must be Pat rising early for band practice at Upper Canada College. He played a small drum and drove us all crazy practising on the arms of the dining-room chairs, or any wooden surface, no matter what else was going on. But never mind, I thought that morning, at last here is someone to talk to. The heavy footsteps came closer and closer, and I peered out of the crack between the door and the wall. But there was no one there! Only the heavy footsteps, too heavy for Pat anyway, and they were somewhere near the bathroom door. Very puzzling.

It was my first encounter of many with the entities, spirits, ghosts who shared 139 with us. Dad had occasionally asked the boys to tread more lightly if they had to come downstairs in the middle of the night, and always each one had denied hopping out of bed.

Mother was adamant that we not talk about the noises, for, as she put it, if we want to sell the house, who would want to buy it with such a reputation? Some years later people recognized the place as haunted. Lucky you if you have not had such an experience. It is always hair-raising, and it was not pleasant to hear those heavy boots trudging about the house with no body attached.

One entity became such a nuisance that Mother asked Father Hutt, rector of St Mary Magdalene's, to exorcise the place. Bell, book, and candle it was. The rector and acolytes trudged around the house. The builder of the neighbouring duplex had come too close to our property line, and the procession had to wiggle its way through. The process alternately fascinated and appalled the neighbours. It worked for a while, but our ghosties turned out to be a hardy lot.

Although the big movie palaces on Yonge Street were out of bounds for my friends and me when we were children, the odd Saturday we did hop on a Yonge streetcar to go and see the latest movie at Loew's or the Imperial. One Saturday, a short featured Mickey Mouse zinging arrows at an apple on somebody's head to the tune of Rossini's *William Tell Overture*. I have no idea what the main attraction was, but the short seemed worth the price of admission. I went home and described the whole thing in great detail, to Dad's obvious amusement. He took me to see *Fantasia* and laughed so hard and so loudly that I wanted to crawl under the seat, especially at the end of Beethoven's Symphony No. 7, when the back end of Pegasus, the flying horse, morphs into a heart. I had one of those awful, "Really Daddy, everybody's looking at us" moments. He became a great Disney fan, particularly of Mickey Mouse. How he would have loved *Sesame Street*!

Charlie Peaker, a good and close friend of Dad's and the organist at St Paul's, frequently stopped by to drive Dad down to the conservatory. Charlie was one of my favourite picker uppers. He had always been reading something interesting the night before and was happy to share some of the nuggets that he had come across. He could quote devastating lines from seventeenth- and eighteenth-century plays: Congreve and Sheridan were favourites. A line in one of Congreve's particularly tickled him, "Your dearth of intelligence, sir, renders you tedious." While he was waiting for Dad one day, he repeated this line to me two or three times; we agreed that this was a quote to savour and both hoped to have an opportunity to use it. I couldn't read yet, so when I came out with the line it had a better effect than I could have imagined. When you have brothers nine, eleven, and thirteen years older than you, it pays to have a few snappy comebacks that stop them short. And the little monster can't even read!

One morning about the same time, an American visitor came to see Dad, a distinguished musician of one sort or another. Dad was busy upstairs, and there was nobody else around. I thought it my duty to entertain him, so I asked him if he would like to hear me recite the alphabet backwards. The brothers had taught me this stunt and thought it side-splittingly funny when I rattled it off at breakneck speed. I guess that my lisp probably added something to the effect. The gentleman was a good audience, thanked me, and gave me a coin for my pains, which turned out to be an American dime, an absolute fortune to me.

This reward opened up a whole new train of possibilities, and I made a habit of asking visitors if they wanted to hear my party piece, the alphabet backwards, for ten cents. It worked like a charm, and I was beginning to feel like a plutocrat until Mother came in one day and interrupted the performance. That was the end of the sideshow.

In the meantime the same three tormentors had taught me Mark Antony's speech from *Julius Caesar* on Caesar's death. It was on the high-school curriculum for one of them, probably Michael. They propped me up on Michael's bed and made a great audience. I declaimed, "Fwenths, Womanth, Countrymen," lisp and all, with fervour. After a few performances, Mother put a stop to my budding career. She thought that the brothers were ridiculing her little daughter. I was furious. Here I had a genuine audience, the brothers rolling around on the floor, holding their sides, wiping their tears, and screaming with laughter, and I just wished that she had minded her own business.

The brothers also passed on to me their knowledge of shooting craps, which, they claimed, they had learned in Sunday School when Dad was still at St Paul's, where they had also picked up a really juicy vocabulary that they eschewed when either of our parents was anywhere near. We played craps for burnt match ends; no one had any money, and I had squirrelled away my hoard of dimes. On Sunday afternoons Dad listened to the New York Philharmonic on the radio upstairs, Mother had a nap, and the coast was clear. At some point Mother must have overheard an enthusiastic, "Come on, snake eyes, my baby needs new shoes!" Or whatever. She came downstairs like a floating fury, wrath personified. Not only were the brothers gambling, but they had included me. It was insupportable. The gambling foray perhaps had the effect of a vaccination on me, as I have never had the slightest interest in any kind of wager.

The summer after my scarlet-fever encounter in early 1927, I had some sort of relapse and had to stay in bed. There was some thought of an operation on a kidney, I think. Dr Harold Ball ('Uncle Harold') prescribed some medicine, horrible stuff, and I refused to swallow it. He came to see me and elected to sit in my room until he decided whether to order surgery or not. I still refused to swallow the medicine. It must have been hours later, after he had tried everything that he knew to convince me to swallow, that he suddenly stood up. He loomed, and I swallowed in a hurry. (He later told me that he had stood up to go home, as it was the middle of the night; but I had thought that he had something more serious in mind.) He said that I had to stay in bed until I could drop a little piece of paper into the bedpan and it turned pink. He gave me a booklet of litmus paper, and I entertained myself testing every liquid that I could find, to see if it were base or acid. Thereafter I never had trouble remembering which was which in chemistry class.

I had great respect for Uncle Harold until he let me down one Sunday morning. A stray kitten climbed up the telephone pole in front of our house, and I started up the pole for the rescue. Every step I took the stupid cat kept going higher. Uncle Harold happened to be driving past. When he saw me not more than 12 or so feet up the pole, he stopped the car, hopped out, and ordered me to come down. I pointed out the kitten's problem and said that I was going after it. We discussed it for a few minutes.

Even though Uncle Harold was wearing his Sunday best – morning coat, top hat, and grey striped trousers, suitable for service as sidesman at St Paul's – we made a deal. If I would come down, he would take my place and go up the pole. He promised, so down I came. He reneged on the deal, saying that the kitten would eventually descend the pole by itself. He returned to his car and sped off to the 11-o'clock service. Oh, the perfidy of adults.

Uncle Harold was such good fun, however, that no one could stay angry at him, and we came to know each other well. Another time I was going home from the library with Nicky on St Clair Avenue. Slowly ascending the hill at Pleasant Boulevard was a Dempster's bread wagon, pulled by what I could see was a bone-weary horse, and the driver was using his whip and yelling at the poor beast. I marched into the middle of the road and told the driver that he should be ashamed of himself for treating his tired horse like that after a long day of dragging the wagon while he sat in comfort. I kept on going until he put the whip away and he told me his name. When I reached home I gave the details to Mother and asked her to phone Dempster's and report that driver. Mother broke up laughing. It seemed that she already knew about the incident. Uncle Harold had witnessed the whole scene and had given her his version of events, but I insisted that it was not funny and that the horse needed protection.

Sometimes I was able to help my mother with her professional endeavours in music. Probably in late 1919, shortly before she had learned that she was pregnant with me, the conservatory had invited her to join the staff. With a rather Victorian flourish, Dad put his foot down – his wife would not work while he was head of the family. Before their marriage they had frequently performed in public together, and now she hid her disappointment. Perhaps he felt a bit threatened, and she knew it. After all, Mother had that imposing degree, and he had none. Perhaps it was just the custom of the times.

However, Dr Vogt was keen to use her talents somehow. So he asked her to write a manual on ear training and sight singing, which she did in 1919 or 1920. Frederick Harris of Oakville published it, and I understand that it was the first such handbook on the subject in North America. Reprints appeared in 1928 with Mother's revisions and in 1939 (see p. 113) and were in use in colleges here and in the United States until the 1940s. A member of the conservatory staff subsequently wrote a textbook on the same subject, cribbing her stuff. Ladies didn't sue for plagiarism in those days. After all, they had acquired the right to vote only a few years earlier.

Mother used me in 1927 as a guinea pig for the revisions. As she intended the book for college students, she figured that if I could work it out, undergraduates should be able to do the same. I could read neither English nor music at that point, so she read out the exercises and asked me to sing or recognize notes, key signatures, and tempi. Sometimes I knew when it was past lunchtime. I was hungry, but she was busy. When I asked about food, she would tell me to forage about in the kitchen for myself and, by the way, make enough for her too. That's one way to learn how to cook, and we had some unusual meals, *nouvelle cuisine* in the raw. She never complained or even suggested improvements or alternatives.

It was in September 1927 that my parents went to a party a little north of the city limits. Randolph Crowe, a young singer who went on to a long and acclaimed operatic career in Greece, had just acquired a Pierce Arrow touring car – a large beast that one could drive with the canvas top down. He was eager to show it off to Dad when he offered to drive my parents to the event.

Everything went well as they cruised up Yonge Street, and the party was a success. But when they were en route home, rain started as they descended the hill into Hogg's Hollow, and the vehicle swerved and skidded. Crowe lost control, and the car left Yonge Street and turned over. The top was still down. The impact threw my father and the driver clear. Dad had only a bad bruise and soreness on his back. His friend Dr Gordon Murray, the eminent surgeon, told him that he was lucky: had the sort of whack he sustained been just an inch or so lower, paralysis could easily have resulted. But the crash trapped Mother underneath the car, with her left arm hanging out. Randolph tried frantically to yank her from the wreckage by her arm, dislocating her shoulder. She had some broken ribs and other damage.

I had been staying with the Ibbetsons, friends of my parents, and their daughter of my age, Jean, at their cottage at Jackson's Point on Lake Simcoe. It was to be for a week, but that week seemed to go on all summer. Finally Mrs Ibbetson told me that Mother was in the hospital, and by the end of the summer I arrived home to find a Miss Fitzpatrick in charge and Dad sad and silent. He was usually so full of fun that this was very concerning. He shipped me off to boarding school at St Mildred's College at Walmer Road and Lowther Avenue. At least there would be no more Whitney.

I begged to see my mother after all these weeks, and finally, as a great indulgence, it happened. Children were not welcome in the adult section at the Toronto General. Dad and I walked down a long hall with a door open at the very end. Mother had both legs tied to some contraption attached to bars suspended from the ceiling, and another one for her arm. I reached the doorway and shrieked. Dad said that they must have heard me across the street in the conservatory, and somebody suggested to Dad, when he or she heard about it, that he might have a Wagnerian soprano on his hands. I imagined that the hospital staff must be torturing Mother – a sort of medieval horror. The visit, a special treat for me, ended abruptly. It took a lot of calm explanation from Dad to convince me that staff members were only trying to make Mother better.

St Mildred's had been a gracious old residence, and then the Sisters of the Church, an Anglican order connected with St Mary Magdalene's, took it over. I became the youngest boarder, taking that honour from my nemesis, the buck-toothed Betty MacDonald, who had gloried in that position. Every night after lights out, Betty used to creep out of bed and cross over to my bed to bite me. There was to be no sound after lights out. Matron was a large and tough elderly party with a grey bun of hair, and there was no fooling around with her: no noise meant no noise, not even a yelp of pain while one was under attack, and Betty knew it.

I waited for revenge. After lunch one day Miss Frankenstein bent over a water fountain downstairs where we boarders weren't to go. The coast was clear, I thought. Betty's bare arm holding down the tap was just too tempting. I bit her hard enough to draw blood. Betty was too surprised to bite back. Unfortunately Sister Sheila, a big wheel in the hierarchy, came around the corner and caught me in the act. She gave me some sort of punishment. But Betty never bit me again. I had already learned from teasing by the brothers that to fight back and win was the way to overcome bullying.

I had another problem with that boarding school. The toilets were archaic. The water closets were near the ceiling, and one operated them by pulling a handle on a long chain. Trouble was, I was too short to reach the handle, so I had to use the more modern facilities in the basement, which were for daygirls only. That meant no access for me after supper, when there were no lights on in the basement. Matron rode her high horse about disgusting people who failed to flush, and she made it clear that she would discover the evil-doer and make her stand up all night in the clothes closet. That terrified me, and I did my best to make my arrangements acceptable to her, but the boarders' toilets didn't even have lids to climb up on. After that bout of scarlet fever, which sometimes results in kidney problems, I was just incredibly lucky.

Walking two by two, crocodile fashion, over to St Thomas' Church on Huron Street before breakfast every morning in Lent didn't endear the routines to me, but I tried to run away only once. Mother had come to pay a call on the school and had taken me out to tea at the Old Mill with the sisters Miss Brush and Sister Teresa, two friends from the Heliconian Club. Teresa Brush had joined the Sisters of the Church and then disagreed with something in the order. She broke away and formed her own one-sister sisterhood, with a new habit of her own design – a big black skirt and a white and brown veil, rather fetching really. It amused her immensely when the hostess at the restaurant changed the record playing of some current fox trot to *In a Monastery Garden*. Back at the school, that little peek at reality and freedom was too much for me, and as the car with Mother and the Brushes left, I took off after it. One of the sisters came galloping after me, so it was back to boarding school for me, and a bite or two after lights out.

No matter how hard I tried in my early years at school, I just couldn't learn to read plain English. They call it 'dyslexia' nowadays. Final examinations were on the horizon; I was eight years old, going on nine, and everyone else in my class at St Mildred's College could read. So far I had bluffed my way through it all with some success, but exams looming made me uneasy. There would be much writing and even reading of the exam questions. Push had come to shove. I asked Mother as casually as possible if there were anywhere in the world where people didn't read. "Oh, yes, dear," Mother replied. "In some remote parts of northern Russia, I believe there are people who cannot read. We call them illiterate."

Great. My heart sank. Russia was not an option. I didn't know a soul in Siberia. Time to take matters into my own hands if the teachers at school couldn't do it. When nobody was around I retrieved

Mother's music, found *Jesu, Joy of Man's Desiring,* and with one finger played the singer's line and studied the combination of letters underneath, saying the words that I knew by memory. It took about a week of practice. I had to be alone in the house, because I didn't want anybody to know of my problem except the housekeeper, and she could keep a secret. At last it all began to make sense.

Time for a test. I dug out Dad's score of *Parsifal,* figuring that I could find a "Dresden Amen" without much difficulty and try to read the words underneath the singer's line. Luckily his score had English as well as German libretti. It worked! Hurrah! Now for the big qualifying exam! Into the kitchen I went, and up onto a shelf in the cupboard. I hauled down cereal boxes and studied the small print. I passed myself. There! That's done. I can read.

Before the duplex at the corner of Inglewood Drive and Clifton Road went up, and many years before the Moore Park Expressway, or Mt Pleasant Road, slashed through the area, the property was a garden for our neighbours Mr and Mrs Cleal on Clifton Road. An American veteran of the Great War, he had left his right arm on a battlefield in France. By hooking a spade or a fork around the stump, he could manage as well as anybody with two arms. I loved to walk along behind him discussing the relative merits of different kinds of corn and tomatoes or watch him harvesting his potatoes. He called me 'carrot top' when Mother wasn't in hearing distance and 'Goldilocks' when she was.

I went to stay with the Cleals for a few days in the summer of 1928 when my parents went to one of the folk festivals that signalled the opening or reopening of one of Canada's magnificent railway hotels. Mrs Cleal let me play with her Raggedy Ann doll – a real one, with a candy heart that you could feel inside her. Mr Cleal took the handle off a six-quart basket, out of which his wife and I made a comfortable bed for my doll, which had never had a bed, and we padded it with pieces from her bag of material scraps. Mrs Cleal could tell me where all the scraps had come from – a portion of a dress that she had made for her daughter when she was a little girl, a piece from her husband's shirt, that sort of thing. In the evening we lighted citronella candles throughout the house to keep the mosquitoes away – a slice of New England life that was new to me and especially delightful.

The Cleals' grandson Teddy Ambridge came to visit one summer, and Mr Cleal prepared a surprise for him. He sawed two-by-fours into six-inch lengths, sanded them smooth, and filled a whole trunk with these 'building bricks.' One afternoon, Mrs Cleal telephoned Mother to ask me over to play with Teddy. It was the first time that I went out on the street by myself, and I was probably about four or five.

Mother, a savvy Londoner, taught me that if a stranger should talk to me I was to say, "I am not allowed to speak to strangers," and then I was to come straight home. "Let me hear you say it," she ordered. I tried it out. "No, no," said Mother. "You must sound much more definite. Let me hear you say it again." I must have been forceful enough, because she let me go around the corner by myself.

Teddy and I had a marvellous time. We each built a tower around ourselves, then used what remained as bombardment to bring down each other's fort. Falling wooden blocks made a spectacular sound. His grandparents in their living-room right below us may have regretted the surprise. Then we built a castle together and argued about the battlements. It was thoroughly satisfying to play with somebody my own size.

Suppertime came, and I started down Clifton Road for home. Just as I reached the corner, an old Pierce Arrow touring car carrying three men came to a stop at the curb; they were all wearing those visor caps that workmen used to sport. The one in the front passenger seat leaned out of the window and asked me, "Would you like a ride in the car, little girl?"

I just repeated the sentence that Mother had taught me in what I figured was a voice in command of the situation, just as I had practised it. The men laughed, but not much – more of a smirk – and the car drove off. Wasn't my Mummy clever, I thought as I climbed up the steps to our house. She had told me exactly how to answer those men, and it didn't occur to me to tell her about it. I had done what she had instructed me to do, and it had worked. I could still pick out that man's face in a police lineup after all those years.

For a few summers Dad was off to teach at various American universities, including two or three seasons at the University of California at Los Angeles. No one used his library/study or paid any attention to it while he was away. Mother was writing a music book for children for Freddy Harris to publish and using the grand piano in the living-room, so Dad's study was free. Like a convert to a new religion, I plunged in, and by the end of the summer I had eaten up all sorts of books, some not quite suitable for children – *The Life of Rabelais,* for instance. That was an eye opener.

There were stacks of poetry books – gifts to Dad, I gathered, from the authors, who hoped that he would set a poem or two. I don't think that he ever did. He taught me to keep a lookout for anything that I thought might be worth setting. "The words must have a good rhythm. There cannot be much sibilance. Whatever it is that the poet is trying to convey must genuinely move you." Those three instructions make an excellent way to enjoy poetry, whether or not it could use music.

Now that reading was no problem for me, I took Nicky for a walk frequently – destination the Deer Park Public Library near St Clair and Yonge. The librarian headed me off to the children's section, but after *Piers Plowman* and *The Life of Rabelais,* no thank you. She now led me to Young Adults; better, but still pretty tame. I helped myself to the adult section. A kindly soul, she relented. I wanted to thank and to greet her by name, but I couldn't remember whether she was Miss Burper or Miss Belcher. The obvious mnemonic is no help in a case like this. She told Mother that her grandfather had been an admiral in the Royal Navy. When I asked Mother which name it was, she said, "Now you have confused me too."

Years later, Dr Gordon Murray remarked that I was ambidextrous, and I found out later still that the ambidextrous frequently find learning to read a daunting task. It also accounted for a slight hesitancy of speech, which we thought hereditary because Dad had it sometimes. When he gave talks on the radio, Mother and I would hold our breath, willing him to handle those trying consonants smoothly. He always did. Dr Hendricks lent Dad a tome called *Disorders of Speech*. I don't think that he ever opened it, but I did. I didn't read beyond chapter 1, but I learned something very helpful. One never stammers while humming or singing, so a stutterer should cultivate an almost-hum on the troublesome consonant, which unsticks the muscles in the throat. With practice, muscles that are taut learn to relax on demand.

I knew that success with this had a lot to do with attitude and learning to relax. Dixon ('Dickie') Wagner, a choir member at St Mary Magdalene's, stammered really badly in ordinary speech, but onstage the stammer disappeared. He 'day jobbed' at Eaton's store in men's wear, but at night he was a fine actor. There just were not opportunities enough for him in Toronto to make acting a paying career.

New houses were under construction near us. Mother and I inspected them on our Sunday-evening walks while Dad played Evensong. The city was paving streets – the 1920s saw expansion and change. The wooden-floored Loblaws on Yonge Street gave way to a new branch on St Clair with bright lighting and a 'magic eye' that opened the door as you passed through – the first that any of us in the neighbourhood had seen. Children now had to sign a book if they bought a bottle of vanilla flavouring – it contained alcohol! Mother sent me to pick up a bottle of flavouring from the little shop at Welland Avenue and Rose Park Drive, a 'mom and pop' establishment. The clerk refused to sell it to me, to Mother's vast annoyance – yet another strange custom of the country that she was trying to understand. Dogs now had to wait outside the stores – no more tidbits from a friendly butcher for a favourite four-legged visitor.

One day a customer outside Loblaws embarrassed Mother to outrage. Noticing her with Nicky as Mother came out of the store with her shopping, the man accosted her and told her bluntly that her dog was a disgrace, the father of his bitch's puppies. What do you say to a charge like that? To cool Mother down, Dad assured her that the fellow was lucky to have so discerning an animal, choosing a first-rate stud for herself and her offspring. The irate owner had presented it as more a case of rape, but heigh-ho, said my father, if you insist on your daughter's remaining virginal, take better care of her. We knew that Nicky had a particular girlfriend, a muscular Great Dane, twice his size. As Dad remarked, there was no accounting for taste in these matters.

In that same Loblaws, Mother frequently noticed another shopper slipping a pound of butter up the wide sleeve of her mink coat, a rarity in the Depression years. Mother knew the manager to speak to. She considered the matter for some days and decided that she should mention it to him. He assured her that he did indeed know about the wide-sleeved lady and her taking ways and that he had an arrangement with her husband. Rather than seeking an embarrassing confrontation, he simply kept track of her pickups and sent the spouse an accounting each month, which he promptly paid. Mother thought it a strange relationship and wondered why the husband didn't buy the kleptomaniac a mink coat with narrow sleeves, except that it wouldn't have addressed the underlying problem.

When sometime in the 1920s the provincial Department of Education engaged Dora Mavor Moore to produce Shakespeare's plays that were on the high-school curriculum, she asked Mother to take charge of music. The players were all high-school students whom Mrs Moore had trained to her exacting professional standards. Young people with dramatic ambitions just naturally floated to her, and many went on to great careers in Toronto, New York, and across Canada, not to mention Hollywood.

Mrs Moore established courses in every aspect of performing. When she needed an extra body to make a class more competitive, she would call Mother to send me over. She held classes in voice production, makeup, mime, whatever she felt would sell. In one of her classes, we each had to warm up by repeating a Gilbert and Sullivan patter song at high speed. It was great training in vocal production. Mrs Moore taught us always to remember that somebody in the back row had given up hard-earned cash to enjoy an evening in the theatre and that it was up to us to make sure that they could hear every word of our part. Wherever she had her studio, there was always a small reproduction of the Chandos portrait of William Shakespeare and, underneath it, a little wooden plaque, the letters burned in, as she in turn burned them into us: "There are no small parts, only small actors."

Mother rarely used more than a piano in those high-school productions – there was no money for more instruments. Performances took place in high schools throughout the city. Some of the auditoria had good facilities, but most did not. In one school, Mother thought that a harpsichord sound would be better than the ratty old upright. She helped herself to a couple of rolls of toilet paper from a washroom and proceeded to thread them carefully in and out around the piano strings while the cast was having its run-through. It seemed an odd thing to do, but Mother's treatment of the old piano made it sound like a fairly respectable harpsichord. Fran Moore, the stage manager, thought it hilarious to see Mrs Willan behind the piano with rolls of toilet paper.

Shakespeare occasionally writes a poem to sing in his plays. Sometimes Mother couldn't find a setting that seemed appropriate or within a young actor's capabilities, or one that didn't require a performing fee (also beyond the budget). She would just ask Dad to set the poem for her. Lo and behold, a setting would appear in no time. One morning at breakfast, when Mother needed a song in *As You Like It,* Dad cautioned her that Mrs Moore's husband, an Anglican cleric and a member of the Arts and Letters Club, was indicating around the luncheon table that his wife was out of her mind, quite mad in fact. Mother was furious. She reminded Dad that Dora had three children to feed and care for. Her husband wasn't much help. As for being mad, she was doing what she had received her training for and had been a success on the Broadway stage. If that were madness, then we were all mad.

Perhaps Dad shared Mother's remarks with his luncheon companions. The Reverend Francis Moore left town shortly afterwards and took up his career in the United States.

It is hard to believe nowadays that in the interwar years women hardly ever divorced their husbands. The laws of the land made it extremely difficult, and Dora Mavor Moore must have been under an enormous strain, financially, emotionally, and socially. She must have had good reason for finally moving against her husband, knowing that people would say slanderous things about her. However, Mother and Dad were on her side. Dad took her work seriously, writing settings for the plays that she was producing and chatting about her accomplishments at the club. Mother was quite angry – her friend was not only *not* mad, but a brilliant director working full time and raising three young sons. Mother's name was on her programs as musical director. These factors may have helped to slow wagging tongues.

Mother was working with her because she was having a wonderful time, making music on her own in the company of a person for whose talents she had the greatest respect and who was moreover a close friend. Mrs Moore's father was a professor of great distinction at the University of Toronto. He was a friend and colleague of George Bernard Shaw's, who named a character after him – the Reverend James Mavor Morell in *Candida*. Professor Mavor, Shaw, and Count Leo Tolstoy all helped to settle the Doukhobours in western Canada.

Professor Mavor was the epitome of the absent-minded professor. Dad described the shenanigans of some of his students one April Fool's Day. They painted a bare foot on each of the professor's rubbers and covered it with black water-colour paint. Then when he walked across the front campus in the rain and the black paint disappeared, it really looked as though he had forgotten his shoes and his socks. Another time Dad regaled Mother with the tale of Mrs Mavor's rushing into his first lecture one morning with his trousers draped over one arm. Her intrusion and her interruption of his lecture surprised her husband. He had bought himself a new pair of trousers the day before and, typically, had neglected to tell her. When she found the old trousers on a chair, she panicked. She claimed later that she just knew that he would forget them one day and really thought that the day had arrived.

Mother took up smoking about 1928. It was the fashionable thing to do. She favoured Bougaslavskys, rather hard to find and with a different smell from ordinary cigarettes. After she had been smoking, I would refuse to kiss her and turn away. Many years later I discovered that I have an allergy to nicotine, but neither of us had known that earlier. Dad smoked a pipe and used tobacco with some sort of flavouring that overshadowed the tobacco smell, and I stayed out of range of that too. Fortunately Dad was never the kissing type of father anyway.

Mother never understood why the Hamlin sisters on the corner of Clifton Road and Glenrose Avenue suddenly cut her dead. She mentioned it only years later. I had to explain and apologize to her. Music publisher Frederick Harris and his wife, Bessie, had invited her to the running of the King's Plate one June when I was about nine. Dad was out of town, and the brothers were nowhere in sight. Mother really wanted to go. She loved horses and good racing, but she asked me over and over if I felt happy about staying at home with only Nicky. I didn't really mind, and she left an early supper for me in case I should become hungry before she returned. So off she went with a light heart in the Harrises' car, with their chauffeur, Collier, at the wheel.

After a while I began to feel a bit bereft, so I took Nicky for a walk around the block. Passing the Hamlins' house, I spotted a strawberry shortcake, an imposing model fit for a wedding reception or a fair, sitting on the windowsill beside their back door. Nicky and I stopped to admire it. One of the Hamlin sisters wanted to know what I was doing alone on the street. I told her that my mother had gone to the races and left me all alone with Nicky. The kindly Miss Hamlin bristled with indignation at Mother's apparent neglect of me and invited us both into the kitchen. She cut a mountainous slice of cake, strawberries galore, whipped cream, a masterpiece. I think that she muttered something about disgraceful goings-on. I thanked her, and Nicky and I resumed our walk. Mother just said, "So that's the reason. Oh well."

Every once in a while in the late 1920s and throughout the 1930s, I attended concerts in Massey Hall. I loved the night ones, when the hired car from Mother's favourite, Deer Park Livery, drove us down the hill on Avenue Road. The lights below always struck me as a sort of fairyland, a prelude to the excitement to follow. Sitting between my parents in the vehicle, with Dad a bit grumpy as he usually was before a performance of one of his orchestral works, I concentrated on the magical sight below us.

At one concert in Massey Hall – probably a student performance – Ernest MacMillan with his wife and sons, Dad, Mother, and I were all in the front row of the first balcony. At intermission, the old people took off for the Green Room, leaving Keith and Ross MacMillan and me by ourselves, an unwise move. Keith chewed the corners of his program into spitballs. Gleefully, with Ross watching, he spat them down to the ground floor, and both ducked in a hurry. Curious as usual, I wanted to see what would happen. A gooey spitball splattered on the top of some poor soul's head. The man looked up and shook his fist at me, when I hadn't done a thing. That taught me something. The brothers, the MacMillan boys, boys in general, had much in common.

Probably it was shortly before the stock-market crash of 1929 that the Moores – Dora, Francis, Mavor, and Peter – moved into an unrestored settler's log house at 2600 Bathurst Street, north of Eglinton Avenue on a bit of a hill. It had a pump for water in the kitchen, no hot water, a wood stove, and outside the kitchen door a beautiful tree, which was a landmark. First Nations people had long ago, when the huge old tree was young, trained one low branch to grow sideways to indicate direction in what was then forest. The log house still exists and may well become part of a museum of the history of Canadian theatre, but the historic tree came down when 2600 Bathurst became an apartment building. Pete and I used to swing on the historic bough.

Fran Moore set to work at once to make the house more comfortable for his mother, installing a bit of plumbing here and there, but the pump was in use for years, and then came hot water out of a tap. Fran was always ingenious in these matters and later studied engineering in Scotland. Many times I sat in the Moores' kitchen, with Dora Mavor Moore perhaps busy using heavy irons heated on the wood stove. At the same time she would be talking about theatre, nonstop, just like music where I came from. Mavor was always trying out production ideas on his mother, some of which died a quick death. She was adamant that unless some stage business advanced the plot or truly illuminated a cloudy point, it had to go, no matter how appealing or attractive for the audience. Mavor always put up a vigorous defence. These discussions sounded like Dad and Mother's, and I felt very much at home.

A big old table across from the stove usually held a dish or two from a previous meal, some from a meal to come, all Quimper ware, the French pottery with two peasants confronting each other. Years later, when the house and tree were no longer there, I came across a Quimper eggcup in an antique shop in Paris's Left Bank. I had to have it, a tangible reminder of halcyon days. Later, in a barn in Quebec's Eastern Townships, I found a cracked, chipped, leaky, and elderly Quimper teapot. Perhaps I paid too much for it. The charming Canadien antique dealer placed into the wrapping a little Quimper sabot, which I found after I returned home.

Up at the Moores', hands were always busy. One summer my friend Joy Kennedy Clarry and I knitted string leggings and tops using needles the size of drumsticks. Then Pete dipped the garments in a pail of aluminum paint and we hung them to dry on the clothesline. Voilà! We had armour for the battle scenes in *Henry V*, the matriculation Shakespeare play that Mrs Moore would be training us for in the coming winter. Joy played the herald. The armour worked beautifully: the actors could move, and their battle gear made no clanks to interfere with actors speaking.

In the Moores' living-room, with warmth emanating only from a fireplace until Fran organized a heating system, a painting of the three boys as small children hung over the sofa. I first knew the boys by their baby names: Fran was Wowie, Mavor was Mame, and Pete was Petey. The room seemed comfortable even in the coldest winter when a noisy, jubilant cast filled it after the end of the run of whatever show we had been putting on.

Early on, 2600 was a primitive dwelling, probably inexpensive – a crucial consideration – but there was a barn on the property! The Barn, as we all knew it, became a theatre right away, with no heating for cold-weather use. Programs of two or three one-acters emerged each summer over many years – an invaluable training ground. There were schoolmates of Mavor's from University of Toronto School; students from Forest Hill Collegiate, where his mother taught theatre in winter; and sons and daughters of her friends – all of us swarming like moths to a fire. It was a delirious place to be, alive with intellectual chatter and an electric sense of achievement.

The 1920s, seemingly carefree despite postwar adjustments, came to a thundering conclusion on Black Monday in October 1929. It was in its way as calamitous and with as far-reaching consequences as any event since, and life changed dramatically for everyone. I don't believe that Dad ever invested in any kind of stocks or even bonds ever again.

PART II

The Warp and Woof of Daily Life

CHAPTER SIX

Family Life at 139

The normal regimen at 139 Inglewood Drive, at least normal to us, apparently struck other people as odd, a bit upside down or back to front. Dad was first one up in the morning. He let out the dog – over the decades Pete, Nicky, Tippy, Chloe, and Trixie – and brought in the newspaper shortly after six. The very early masses at St Mary Magdalene's in Holy Week were nothing awkward for him. He read the paper – the conservative *Mail and Empire* when Toronto had two morning journals, and after it merged with the liberal *Globe* in 1936 he gradually adapted to the new *Globe and Mail*. He always checked the cricket scores and finished the crossword puzzle. Mother was in charge of breakfast; after the accident that injured her and sent me off to boarding school in 1927, we had a series of housekeepers; Mother took over again when the Depression began to hit hard and housekeepers became instead non-resident cleaning ladies.

At the breakfast table, a hideous ceramic dish featured fake white basketry, pink roses, and a couple of bluebirds; we nicknamed it 'the birdbath,' a trophy from a church bazaar at St Mary Magdalene's. This treasure held plum jam or orange marmalade – Mother made both – and Dad used a tablespoon to dish it onto his toast. Our one little plum tree, a relic from a forgotten orchard on the site, outdid itself year after year. The brothers propped up the branches after they became so heavy with fruit that they collapsed onto the ground. For several days in the hottest August weather, Mother wrestled with that little tree's harvest. The result lasted usually until February, when Seville oranges would arrive. Each batch of marmalade took three days to prepare and a lot of patience, along with knowing the exact moment to take the rich, scented, simmering pot off the heat. Mother's product was a dead ringer for Cooper's Oxford marmalade, the brand of choice at the time.

We also had a cherry tree, but I don't remember that we ever had anything from it. The robins beat us to it every year. Bunny tried a variety of tricks to outwit them, but robins prefer cherries unripe and sour. One year he covered the entire tree with cheesecloth, but a crafty bird made a hole and invited his whole tribe to come on in. They could not find the exit and raised a shrieking ruckus in noisy protest. We still didn't have a cherry. Every single one had a bite out of it.

The only other leftover from the orchard was an apple of indeterminate lineage, a tree that had no idea that it should not grow into the size of a mature maple. Sometime in the 1920s a .22 rifle mysteriously appeared, and the brothers entertained themselves by climbing 20 feet or so up the tree for a better viewpoint to shoot squirrels. They never managed to hit anything of consequence, fortunately, or anything moving, but after justifiable complaints from neighbours the rifle just as mysteriously disappeared. Tippy, the fox terrier who succeeded Nicky in 1938, had the most fun with that tree. He fancied himself a climber, and at a few words of encouragement up he would go – it was his party piece.

Before I left for school each morning, when I was not boarding, I said "Goodbye" to Mother at one end of the table and walked to Dad's end, so he could examine my appearance from top to toe. I never could figure out how he could do it so fast, but I often had to go back upstairs to brush hair, clean teeth, polish shoes, clean finger nails, whatever was not up to his standards. He despised long fingernails, calling them "claws" and unbecoming. Mine had to be short. It didn't matter that I was not studying to play the organ. If I didn't keep them short, we would have a nail-trimming session. I preferred to look after my nails myself.

Toronto critics were frequently the subject of Dad and Mother's own comments at the breakfast table, a source of amusement to them, as well as of irritation. Musicians, like actors, generally think poorly of critics. George Bernard Shaw remarked that those who can do, those who can't teach, and those even lower become critics, even though he was a music critic himself.

My parents agreed with Shaw. They reserved their particular disdain for Lawrence Mason, the mean-spirited, if brilliant (PhD from Yale), critic on the *Globe*, before it merged with the *Mail and Empire* to become the *Globe and Mail*. The Dickens Fellowship, a group of professional men who held dinners with a speaker and who obviously knew little about music, invited Dr Mason to speak at a gathering. He arrived, ate his dinner, listened to an introduction, stood up, and said, "Thank you for dinner." He walked to the cloakroom, retrieved his hat, and left the hall. The musicians in the crowd chortled and guffawed; any one of them could have told the members not to ask Mason to do anything. It probably remains as the shortest after-dinner speech anywhere.

The critic's unspeakable behaviour did nothing for his reputation. For the conservatory, Dalton Baker acquired a poster-size picture of the Pre-Raphaelite Holman Hunt's *The Light of the World*, a painting of Christ holding a lantern in one hand and facing the viewer while knocking on a massive door obscured by tendrils. He pasted a picture of Mason's face on top of Christ's, glued a big sign 'MASSEY HALL' on the door, and then, for the coup de grâce, retitled the picture *Behold I Stand at the Door and Knock*. He thumb-tacked his masterpiece on the bulletin board, and the result was sensational. Some people laughed uproariously, claiming that Mason deserved it; Dad, with a twinkle in his eye, reported that others "showed shock and consternation." Most of the denizens of musical Toronto considered the parody both apt and witty.

Few mourners attended Mason's funeral in 1939. His brother came from Boston to carry back his ashes to inter in the family plot there. After the service, the reluctant sibling took off for Union Station to catch the next train back home. He must have placed the urn beside him on a bench while waiting and fallen asleep or been reading a book. When the Boston train was ready, he ran to it, leaving the ashes behind. There was speculation for some time in the giggling musical community. Did the railway auction Mason off at an unclaimed-goods sale? Did someone lay him to rest in a pauper's cemetery? Dr Mason's brother never showed up to retrieve the urn.

There were other music critics in town. Augustus Bridle, on the *Toronto Daily Star*, was a source of constant amazement to both of my parents. 'Gus,' as members knew him in the Arts and Letters Club, invented a stream-of-consciousness style all his own. It dispensed with verbs here and there and relied greatly on dashes. "Whatever does he mean?" Mother would ask. "Hanged if I know," Dad would answer. Bridle was conscientious about sitting through performances and reporting promptly, but musicians generally wished that he was not so obscure. He really was a conundrum.

Rose MacDonald wrote for the *Evening Telegram*. She never learned to type, but colleagues said that her handwriting was impeccable, with never a crossed-out word or phrase. She obviously enjoyed good music performed well, listened intelligently, and knew how to write things up, which won her the respect of her readers, including musicians.

The *Globe and Mail* had Pearl McCarthy, whom Dad always referred to as 'Priceless Pearl.' Her criticisms and her opinions won respect. She was a great friend of cellist Leo Smith and his wife, Leila, and wrote a biography (1956) about him after his death in 1952. Leo Smith was first cello of the Toronto Symphony Orchestra and had a distinctive way of playing. Some people said that he looked as though there was a bad smell coming out of his instrument; others suggested that it might be the resin that he used on his bow.

Most evenings we had dinner without Dad, but Saturday night was special. Dessert was always vanilla ice-cream and little sponge cakes shaped like miniature loaves of bread. These treats arrived at dinner-time, at first from George Coles and later from his son Walter, when he took over the business. That was Dad's favourite dessert, and there was no variation.

Just about dinnertime that evening, *Saturday Night* reached subscribers' doors thanks to the aptly named Red Rocket wagon, wheeled along by a young man with some sort of disadvantage. Dad always wanted to know what Hector Charlesworth, the music critic, had to say. They were friends at the Arts and Letters Club. That gentleman looked very much like King Edward VII – the same portliness, goatee, general appearance, and air of stating universal truth. He loved to hear about this resemblance. His reviews were rather lofty in tone, as I remember. But Dad told me that after a good dinner at the club and post-dinner refreshment, Hector liked to sing his favourite tune, the "Triumphal March" from *Aïda*, beating time with whatever weapon was at hand on the arm of his chair. Dad grinned with a merry twinkle in his eyes when he told me this. I think he enjoyed the fact that his old friend had some more informal tastes than his erudite views for publication would suggest.

Sunday was very much a working day. The housekeeper prepared breakfast for Dad, while Mother and I went to early service, with breakfast for us afterwards in the church basement. The smell of white bread toasted and tea haunts me still. I then went to Sunday School, and Mother chatted with friends. The Sisters of the Church, from the convent next door, taught Sunday School. My place was beside Hugh Stiff, later a bishop. We egged each other on, to the despair of the sister trying to teach us something. All in all, Sunday School was not a great success with the brothers or me.

Dad arrived at church well before 11 o'clock to assemble his choirs, and Mother and I took off for home, except on high festival Sundays, when we attended both services. Sunday dinner was usually at about two o'clock. Sometimes Dad stayed after the service to chat with visitors, from out of town, even out of country. There was one intrepid soul – we never learned his name – who at least once a year dropped a $100 U.S. bill in the collection plate and drove a Cadillac with Texas licence plates to hear Dad play. This in the days when a motor trip to Buffalo was quite an undertaking. It must have been a sort of pilgrimage for him.

After dinner on Sundays, Dad listened to the New York Philharmonic on the radio at high volume. In warm weather, with our windows open, the whole neighbourhood heard it too. I liked to listen with him, and his comments on the comments of Deems Taylor were illuminating. Taylor once described a work of Tchaikowsky's – one of the symphonies – as banal, and my father jumped straight up out of his chair. "He is wrong, WRONG, wrong," Dad snarled. "Tchaikowsky is NEVER banal," he affirmed, going straight to a bookcase filled with miniature scores. He found the relevant passage. "He is wrong. He hasn't paid close attention to the score," and Dad hummed the melody as written, keeping time by waving the score around. Dad knew that the conductor, by strictly observing what the composer had written and presumably intended, could with a subtle change in emphasis, a slight change on one note, or a small hesitation transform a few notes in a pleasant progression into a statement of utmost pathos.

When Giles Bryant and I were working on the catalogue of Dad's compositions for the National Library of Canada after my father died in 1968, I remarked that when Elmer Iseler and all the other conductors performed Dad's motet *Hodie, Christus natus est* (c. 1935), it just simply lacked the punch that I remembered my father's giving it; there should be a pause after "Hodie," a syncopation. Giles seized the copy, pushed his glasses off his nose, and peered closely. "You're right," he said. "There IS a dot after the 'Hodie.' There should be a pause." It changes what you hear completely.

In about the same era as his outburst at Deems Taylor, Dad had been in New York and had run into John Barbirolli, recently arrived from London to be conductor of the New York Philharmonic. He came from a musical family that Dad had known in England, his father a violinist and John first a cellist. Barbirolli recounted his first few days in the United States – rehearsing the orchestra long and hard, stepping out for the quickest lunch, and finding a pleasant enough little place around the corner that sold little round buns with a hole in the centre, greasy and sugary but tasty. Then someone informed him that doughnuts and coffee for lunch every day was not a good way to stay healthy. Barbirolli laughed at his own naïveté when telling my father the story, and Dad laughed when he shared it with me.

Teatime on Sunday was special. It was an occasion for friends to drop in: sometimes Dad invited students, which Mother encouraged, or a musician or two from other parts of the world who had been to St Mary's in the morning and would accompany Dad to Evensong. Our parents expected the four of us young people to be present and to be on our best behaviour.

For that tea, Mother liked to bake a layer cake and ice it. She then gave me free range to decorate it with nuts, cherries, whatever was handy and to make patterns with a variety of cookies on another plate. Sometimes after Dad had left for evening service, we had a string quartet of students going, or a quintet with Mother at the piano. When tea was over, Dad had left, and the boys were off on their own concerns, Mother would occasionally play a whole recital, piano alone or accompanying herself in her medal-winning mezzo. Her particular favourites were Dvořák's *Biblische Lieder* and Bach's *Jesu, Joy of Man's Desiring*. The Bach was such a regular on the program that I eventually tired of it. I had memorized both words and melody, which proved very handy in my self-education.

Mother asked me during these private recitals to guess composer, key signature, tempo. Perhaps she thought that I would become the soloist that she could so easily have been. She tested me on style recognition. She often played Chopin's *Fantaisie*, Opus 49, and I bit every time, guessing Schumann or maybe Schubert, close but not close enough, the right century anyway. "You must try to remember what you are taught," she would say, a reflection of her frustration with her non-musician-to-be student.

Every June we had a visitor for at least one dinner who was a favourite with the whole family. George Wilson was music supervisor for the high schools in all of Brooklyn. He must have been a Republican, because he believed firmly that President Franklin Roosevelt was out of his mind, and his comments about Eleanor, the first lady, were disparaging, to put it mildly. He told outrageous jokes in his wonderful Brooklyn accent all through dinner. His parlour trick was to walk up and down stairs in a funny shuffle that was a fine takeoff on Charlie Chaplin. Each year after dinner we begged him to do the Charlie Chaplin shuffle.

He was so complimentary about the meal the first year he came that Mother repeated the menu year after year, year after year. Each time he would roll his enormous eyes and smack his lips. It seemed as though he waited breathlessly all year long for dinner with us. Poached Restigouche salmon and cucumber sliced in a vinegar sauce brought him almost to tears of pleasure.

Mr Wilson kept returning because if he acquired a doctorate of music his salary would increase dramatically. Each year Dad failed him in his *viva voce* exams, and each year he determined to try harder. Mother asked Dad once why he couldn't just take pity on the poor soul and give him his coveted doctorate. We were in the kitchen at the time. "He has no more music in him than – " Dad searched for an object, "that basket." It was the six-quart container in which Mother kept her tools – hammers, screwdriver, chisel, pliers, whatever she needed for a household repair. (Mr Parsons, who owned the hardware store on Yonge Street below St Clair, always sold her top of the line, so the contents of the basket were all first class.) Mr Wilson retired eventually, still without his Mus. Doc. There were very few universities offering such a degree in the 1920s and early 1930s.

Toronto was the handiest for him apparently, and the most prestigious for his purpose.

Christmas was a splendid feast time in our house, as we honoured old-country customs. On the Sunday before Advent, in early November, the collect for the day begins: "Stir up we beseech thee, O Lord, the wills of thy faithful people." Stir-up Sunday was the signal to start on all the special baking and preparations.

Mother used to go to Michie's on King Street with a formidable shopping list in hand. On a few Christmases before I started school I went with her. Michie's had stools in front of the counter so that ladies could perch in comfort while discussing their orders with Mr Michie. As well as offering dried and candied fruits for the cake and puddings, he had cheeses from France, Germany, and Holland, most of them only at Christmastime, crackers, and pickles from England, including pickled walnuts, Dad's favourite. The walnuts were to go with the inevitable meals of cold turkey, along with Mother's favourite Turkish Delight and so many packages, tins, and boxes. In due course the store would deliver the order, and unpacking it was so much fun.

The season really was a time of preparation. Mother made vast amounts of fruit cakes and plum puddings, and each and every one of us had to have a stir, including the people who worked for us – the general housekeeper and the man who tended the coal furnace every morning. Before Mother wrapped the puddings in linen jackets for steaming, she would clean and shine a ten-cent piece to place inside the New Year's Day pudding. Whoever received the coin would have good luck for the coming year.

In England people used a sixpence. Mother recalled the same customs in her own childhood home and Grandpapa's presiding over a huge, fresh Stilton cheese. He would run a special copper wire this way and that through the cheese wheel to make those blue veins, the only time apparently he entered the kitchen, but he probably had to give the pudding mixture a stir like everybody else. The entire household – cook, maids, family – had to stand by and observe his manoeuvre.

St Mary Magdalene's Church was widely known in the 1920s and early 1930s for its Christmas Pageant. Dad would arrange several carols, and Sunday School students would take parts. I was always an angel; my long blonde hair won me the part I suppose, but I never made the star roles of Joseph or Mary.

Dinner on Christmas Eve was simple and quiet. We had already decorated the tree, and the candles in their metal clamps on the boughs were ready for lighting the next day with a match. Dad was in charge of that. Everybody had an evening nap, with interruptions from many people calling to ask about the time for the service. Finally the time arrived to wake up and set off for church. Dad left early. The choir had to be in place well before the service began. Travelling through the city at night, with snow falling or piled up helping to deaden sound, we would pass houses with just one light or two on, or no lights. The experience was mysterious, like taking the wheel on a ship on dog watch, with everyone asleep, feeling apart from the ordinary world, something quite special.

The church always had a crowd, and people pushed chairs close together. Even so, there was standing room only for many worshippers. Latecomers crammed into the narthex, and it was a long service, as many people took communion. There was usually a new carol. Year after year Mother said the same thing. "Listen very hard to this one. It's the first time the choir has sung it, and quite the best carol your father has written."

It seemed as though musical Toronto turned out in its hundreds to that special occasion. Dad extemporized at every service but that one. He anticipated, with seemingly no break in a variation or a melodic line, the precise moment when the procession would reach a specific place, so that the congregation could burst into the next verse of a hymn down to the second. Dad playing virtually non-stop, the scent of incense, and the *sfumato* effect of its smoke, as well as what was going on in the chancel, brought out a complete silence from all the people packed in together, a palpable reverence.

After the midnight service I stood beside Mother, shaking hands dutifully with strangers who all seemed to know me and to be complimentary about the music. I later learned that some of these people had come from New York and beyond. For them it was a sort of pilgrimage. Being sleepy or feeling grumpy was not on. Mother made it very clear that it was my duty to respond with politeness and grace – a very useful lesson and a good habit.

Then the choir members came to our home for a party, which went on for the rest of the night – the most joyous part of the whole week. They had all worked hard, not just at St Mary's but at concerts and recitals in a choir, the Mendelssohn and others, including performing several *Messiahs*. The party allowed them to let off steam, but Dad was exhausted, although he never admitted it.

When the choir arrived, hungry and thirsty, participants often played carols – on beer bottles! If one drinks the right amount and breathes out across the neck of the bottle – a bit like playing a flute – it makes a mellow sound, with the level in the bottle determining the note. This takes a lot of fine tuning, with the occasional, "Oops, best finish this one off and try again." Or one might use a crystal glass with just the right amount of liquid, which makes a ringing, high-pitched tone when one rubs the rim quickly with a finger. The effect was both hysterical and magical.

Robert Fleming, one of Canada's gifted composers, had a wonderful party piece, his one-minute opera. He thwacked out appropriate chords and howled, yodelled, and growled his way through an improbable and atrociously stupid plot, falsetto, basso, and in between, with a word or two, in great seriousness explained the plot. It was side-splittingly funny and as melodramatic as only opera can be. Eventually there would be performances of Dad's carols and others.

Listeners washed down these musical treats with Mother's trifle. A wall of lady fingers lined Grandmama's punch bowl, which contained whipped cream, whatever else goes into a trifle, and dollops of sherry, but not enough to make it soggy like most trifles. I decorated the whole according to my own design, with red candied cherries, angelica strips, and shelled almonds. Mother's trifle was famous. She didn't have a recipe; she just made it to taste the way she remembered it from home in England. I have no idea how she did it.

Grandmama's punch bowl had a silver rim. Bunny loved to paint. He did the bathroom in a deep pink and the throne a silver colour with aluminum paint, which took hours to dry, to everyone's discomfiture. But his rendering the rim of Grandmama's punch bowl baby blue was too much. It took me ages to remove that paint.

Many of Dad's students came from so far away that a Christmas trip home would have been impractical or impossible. Mother urged Dad to gather them up and bring them to Christmas dinner at 139. It was quite common for us to have four, five, or more young people whom we had never met share that special meal with us, which made it all the more fun.

We never knew what time we would be eating. It all depended on Norman Wilks, who both taught piano and travelled around the world giving recitals. Mrs Wilks lived in London, and her husband in Toronto. They saw each other only when he happened to be in London performing in Wigmore Hall. Norman Wilks had been in the front-line trenches in the Great War. Every Christmas morning he went to play at Toronto's Lambert Lodge, where badly wounded veterans were staying for life. Then he asked the men for requests and kept on playing for as long as anybody could think of a song or a tune that they wanted to hear. Sometimes dinner was around three, sometimes well after four. It didn't matter, we waited for Norman Wilks.

One year a student of Dad's, Norah Willis, brought her special friend, a law student, both of them from the west. She had a Christmas present for me, which I thought very kind, as I had never met her before. It was an Eaton Beauty doll with a wonderful gown of a flowered brown silk that shimmered, really lovely. At dinner I sat next to her, and she asked me if I had noticed that the doll's dress matched her own. I had noticed that my new doll was wearing an exact miniature of her gown. For once in my life I had no words, only an emphatic nod. Then she said that since my doll and she were wearing identical dresses and she had made them both herself, that made us relatives of a sort and that I was to call her 'Aunt Norah.' She married her special friend, Roland Michener ('Uncle Roly'), and Dad wrote *Epithalamium* (1948) especially for the wedding of their daughter Joan.

The Christmas after the accident with Randolph Crowe's car, Mother was still a recovering invalid. Dad decided that he would spare her the effort and instead organize Christmas dinner at the Walker House, on the south side of Front Street, west of York Street. We had a private dining-room, a pleasant place in a pale green, quite pretty I thought. There were several students, Norman Wilks of course, and a cousin or two of Dad's from British Columbia. Things were rather elaborate. Mother had warned me about cutlery: "Just start at the outside and work your way into the middle," but there were a lot of forks and knives.

Our waiter was serving the pudding and put my plate down in front of me. I remarked to him, in confidence I thought, that this dinner must be costing my father a lot of money. He suddenly took himself off to the sideboard to do something, turning his back to us, and his shoulders really shook. He recovered after a while, thank goodness, and continued to pass the plates of pudding. I'm afraid that other people overheard my comment and found it amusing.

Horses drew carts of all sorts to make deliveries. Our milkman, Mr Saunders, brought us milk, cream, and butter in time for breakfast every day but Sunday. When snow covered the streets, the squeaky sound of his sleigh along with the clop, clop of his horse meant that you had only minutes for a quick snuggle under the eiderdown before it was time to be up and doing.

I used to keep an ear alert to hear Miss Fitzpatrick, or Fitz, go down to the kitchen. I gave her a little time to put the kettle on and then, in my dressing gown, tiptoed down to join her. We drank tea together, mine mostly milk, and ate thin slices of toasted brown bread, on which we spread dripping very thinly. Dripping is the juice in the roasting pan and the serving dish – no flour, just juice and a little fat, a bit salty – that the cook saves and stores in the refrigerator. What a way to start a winter's day, dark and silent outside, but being cosy and warm at the kitchen table with a friend. We discussed everything, whatever came into our heads. One day Dad realized that I had quite unconsciously picked up a real Glaswegian accent. There was only one place that I could have acquired it. Fitz had to go. She was my friend, and I missed her very much.

Mr Saunders worked for the Acme Farmers Dairy, a good old Toronto firm. His employer must have wondered once a week what took him so long to finish his rounds. He visited homes too early to collect then, so periodically at the end of his rounds he returned to collect money and take orders for any change in the daily routine – perhaps extra cream and butter if a customer were entertaining, more milk if young cousins were visiting.

Mr Saunders was a lonely Londoner, a real East End Cockney. As soon as he caught Mother's accent from London, though a long way from the sound of Bow Bells, he started chatting with her. Sometimes they talked for an hour or more. I think that Mother learned a great deal about life in her hometown about which she had known nothing. I asked her why she didn't just tell Mr Saunders that she was busy and shut the door on him, but her answer was that he was so very lonely and just wanted to talk to someone who could picture what and where he was coming from.

One day he showed his most prized possession to her, a gold sovereign, a coin of the value of twenty shillings, or a pound, but rare indeed. His mother, he told her, had worked in a West End gentlemen's club, so, after the members had called it a night, she had to stay to clean up ashes in fireplaces, empty cigar trays, and tidy up in the kitchen. At the time of his story, she already had four children and was pregnant. As she was walking across town to reach home very early one morning, she passed yet another such club with a group of drunken rowdies stumbling down the steps. One overweight individual lost his footing, bumped into her, and knocked them both flat into the curb. At once someone helped him up, and another reveller took her name and her address.

Next morning, when she had only roused the children and fed and dressed them for the day, two men came puffing up the stairs to her flat and rapped on her door. It was the man who had knocked her down the night before and his friend who had taken her name. The overweight one apologized and, according to Mr Saunders's account, really seemed to mean it. He wanted to know how many children she had and hoped that she would forgive him and accept these portraits of his mother, laying five gold sovereigns on her table, including one for the little one on the way.

She never considered spending them. In fact, who in that neighbourhood would think that she had come by them honestly? Each of her children received a memento of the day when the Prince of Wales (later King Edward VII) arrived at her home and apologized. Mr Saunders always carried his coin safe in an inside pocket.

During the Depression, few people had cash. Anyone throwing money around recklessly would have been a trifle suspect – a little bootlegging on the side, perhaps? For playing at weddings, Dad often received a gift rather than a fee. It sometimes did occur to Mother to wonder if it was a duplicate or some gift that the bride did not want.

One such payment was a little wooden mantel clock. After a while it just stopped, and to our astonishment Dad elected to fix it. He spread out newspaper and systematically began spreading its innards on the paper in strict order of removal. I had never seen him handle a screwdriver before. Mother watched in fascination or amusement, possibly both. At some point he figured that he must have corrected the interplay of its little wheels and screws, and he put everything back very methodically in the same order, or so he thought. He wound it up and set the hands. The hands began to move – backwards. Dad just shrugged, and we all applauded. The clock went back on the mantelpiece solely because it was a pretty little thing, though useless. Visitors who noticed it always did a double take.

Dad's only hobby, I think, was philately, and he did have an impressive stamp collection. The brothers all took it up in the lower grades at school, and so, much later, did I. I gathered the leftovers by ransacking every waste-paper basket, especially Dad's. As the brothers were at school all day, I had first pickings after Dad had taken the best bits, and then one by one the boys tired of sorting little bits of paper and sticking them into an album. Pat gave me his whole collection, traders and all, as well as his catalogue, so I could begin in earnest. Now I could track down the identities of the portraits, the maps, scenic bits. It was fun.

When the centennial of Dad's birth rolled around in 1980, the Canadian postal service acknowledged it with a stamp, which showed a photograph of Dad in front of the organ at St Paul's, perhaps the first time that an organ had appeared on a Canadian postage stamp. First-class mail cost 17 cents in 1980!

Dad told me one day about his father's collecting in London – brass candlesticks. Apparently on Saturday mornings he would poke around in Oxford Street antique shops, Portobello Road, and even junk shops in the East End, with Dad, then a small child, in tow. There was one store that he favoured, and he often discussed his hobby with the owner. Dad and the owner's son had eyed each other coldly. Dad laughed about it when he told me. The little boy grew up to be Joseph Duveen, Lord Millbank, an art dealer who persuaded American millionaires into parting with unheard-of sums for European old masters. Altman, Frick, Kress, Mellon, Morgan, and Rockefeller were among his best clients. S.N. Behrman wrote a biography, *Duveen*, and Dad, in the copy that he gave me, described the subject as a "fascinating rascal": "It gives, to me at all events, some of the hitherto un-understandable reasons as to the astounding prices paid for certain pictures ... here it is with my love."

The men at the Arts and Letters Club loved my father's limericks, but Mother and I never seemed to hear them. Keith MacMillan collected a number of Dad's and others' and published them in a book. It was the first time that Mother or I had come across any of them. Dad did repeat a quatrain for me at one point. I don't know whether he wrote it or not, but it could easily be his own. "King David and King Solomon led very naughty lives / With various kinds of vices and various kinds of wives / But when they felt death coming on with various types of qualms / King Solomon wrote the Proverbs and King David wrote the Psalms."

Like the English divine whose name they bear, Dad occasionally lapsed into unpremeditated spoonerisms. One evening at dinner he told Mother and me that he had been walking that morning from the streetcar on College Street to the front door of the conservatory. Right behind him and missing him by inches, a shattering crash sent glass and pieces of a couple of automobiles flying everywhere. He reached Miss Bath at the registrar's desk and was recounting to her his frightening experience and narrow escape. He was going to end the account with the words "both cars were shattered to bits," but that was not the way it came out. Apparently everyone within earshot was helpless with laughter. That one travelled all over town.

Miss Lillian Bath was both Ernest MacMillan's secretary and the conservatory's registrar – probably a prototype for the 'girl Friday' epithet. Whenever one of my parents dumped me with her, she entertained me on her typewriter. She made long lines of upper- and lower-case Os, quotation marks, slants, brackets; she used the whole top row of the keyboard and produced lines of soldiers, cats, and monkeys. She could also type rhythmically – waltzes, foxtrots, minuets, marches, almost anything that you asked for. Miss Bath was a creative wonder.

In her will she left me an engraving of Landseer's *Distinguished Member of the Humane Society* – I think that was its name – a lovely, noble Labrador with paw nonchalantly over the edge of something. I treasured it. One day it simply walked out of the house while I was in school. I never found out what happened to it. Somebody else must have valued it too. Such is life.

CHAPTER SEVEN

Humane Society Outpost

Caring for animals must run in our family. Miss Loring and Miss Wyle – 'The Girls' – were great animal lovers, and we got along with them very well. I was on Miss Loring's team for the Humane Society tag day, and she encouraged me to take Nicky along as a silent witness.

The Christmas of 1924, when Nicky arrived – a tiny, fluffy, black-and-white puppy that Dad picked up in the St Lawrence Market as Pat's present – Mother and Dad had some friends in for a drink. They placed three or four empty bottles in a six-quart basket for the garbage pickup. Nicky could just reach the necks of the bottles by putting his front paws on the basket rim. He licked them clean, staggered down the hall, and collapsed in the middle of the living-room carpet, out cold for a couple of hours.

Thereafter Nicky was a teetotaller until his first heart attack 14 years later. Mother called the veterinarian, who advised warm milk with a touch of brandy. Nicky had three more heart attacks in quick succession. Mother omitted the brandy after the fourth attack. The dog had been an actor all his life, but those heart attacks were his best performance.

Nicky's second Christmas had its dramatic moments too. We had our usual crackers, going off with several bangs. Nicky managed to escape outside and took off, frightened and confused, up Inglewood Drive, across St Clair Avenue – not very busy on Christmas Day, thank goodness – and up Inglewood's north end, to the last house, where Michael's friend Chassie Martin lived. Chassie's dog, Bimbo, large and friendly, had a good relationship with Nicky. He was a Kentucky red-bone hound with a red mouth; the family claimed that his bones really were a reddish colour. Nicky whimpered at the Martins' door for help. They let him in, and he cuddled up with Bimbo. The Martins telephoned us, and Pat, the nominal owner, and Michael had to go at once and collect him. The Martins were in the middle of their Christmas dinner too. Dad decreed that there would never be another cracker in the house, and there never was.

One Sunday after church, Dad had some errand at the conservatory. When he stepped out onto College Street, he noticed a low-flying pigeon being hit by a driver who did not stop. I have heard that Dad stopped traffic and rescued the bird, carrying it to the door of the conservatory and then calling the Humane Society. It was as if people thought us a northern branch of the local Humane Society, as they would bring injured birds, squirrels, cats, and dogs to our door. We just called the Humane Society, wondering why these people could not do the same thing themselves. When a dog suddenly appeared on the living-room's outside windowsill with a gentle yap to alert somebody to open the window so he could leap down into the room, they looked uneasy. Nicky preferred leaping up on the porch wall and doing a little jump in midair to reach the windowsill to just barking at the front door. That dog had what theatre people call 'presence,' and he knew how to make an entrance. It all seemed quite normal to us, but I can still remember people's eyes opening wide.

We heard wonderful tales of Nicky's acting abilities. One time the Laileys next door were laughing uproariously when they passed Nicky going at it, digging a hole in the Butlers' front garden three doors down as though he had unearthed a pot of gold or an over-ripe steak. Nicky had injured his right paw a few days prior and was making the most of a dramatic limp and words of sympathy. When someone asked, "How is Nicky with the poor, sore paw?" he could look pathetic, holding up the paw for more attention. So, of course, one of the Laileys asked the relevant question. At once Nicky dug just as furiously with his left paw but held the right with great care and tenderness, and it hardly touched the hole. "This dog is a fraud," they said. "No, no," we replied, "that dog is an actor."

Pat's love for transient animals extended to the organ-grinder's monkey. We never knew his name, but he and Pat trusted each other. He made a chittering sound if anyone else approached too close, but Pat could stroke his back and tickle his neck, and the monkey showed his teeth as though he were smiling. Mother of course always had to supply the coin for Pat to present to his pal. The monkey put it between his teeth before he handed it over to his boss.

Pat's school friend Reg Hunt lived a few doors up the street from us. His father owned Hunt's Bakery, which made cakes as well as great ice-cream. Mr Hunt, like almost everyone else, was converting to motor vehicles and sent his horses to pasture but gave one to Reg. After a lifetime of dragging carts around, Reg's was only too glad to hang up his harness and take it easy. Reg stabled him in the Eglinton Hunt Club stables on Avenue Road just north of Eglinton Avenue. Open fields surrounded the clubhouse, whence the well-to-do members hunted on horseback, pink coats and all. The fields were so open that Upper Canada College, where the brothers studied, had a cross-country race over them each autumn. The boys ran straight out of their grounds and up past Eglinton Avenue over hill and dale, circling back to the school. The rather large woman who ran the school tuck shop, 'Sophie Tucker' to the boys, made cakes that went on plain white ceramic plates to each form's fastest runners. Pat mounted his plates on his bedroom wall with a suitable inscription about times and dates.

Reg's horse, like any other, needed exercise. Reg had to go up to the Hunt Club regularly and saddle him up, and Pat frequently went with his friend, probably to take out another horse that needed a gallop. The fun was to back Reg's out of his stall; the creature was adamant – galloping around was not on, thank you. All that Reg had to do was to say to him loudly, "All right for you. You are going back to the bakery." The animal understood every word; he would back up gracefully and lower his head for the bit and bridle as if to say, "Oh, all right. You've made your point."

Michael had a pet too. Her name was Rosy, a white rat with red eyes. Mother tolerated Rosy because the creature loved music. When Mother played the piano, Rosy unlatched the catch of her cage and came to sit right behind the pedals. She loved Schumann and Schubert, but Mozart sent her into a blissful rat heaven, her little paws limp across her chest or thoughtfully stroking her whiskers. As Dad put it, Rosy has taste. She enjoyed Debussy, but Mozart really was the hit on her parade.

Rosy must have arrived *enceinte* and produced a little family, but she wasn't into motherhood. Her indifference so disturbed Mother that she emptied the rubber sack of a Parker fountain pen, filled it with milk, and fed the babies. It took her all morning. Rosy watched with interest but curled up and fell asleep. Wet nursing a bunch of rats became too time consuming for Mother. The rat babies disappeared after a couple of days, and for Rosy life returned to normal. Fortunately the unmotherly rat had no further opportunities to produce offspring. It seemed that music was her sole passion.

Even the neighbourhood dogs seemed to know of our reputation as an unofficial outpost of the Humane Society. One very cold winter night, the temperature well below zero in the old Fahrenheit reckoning (minus 20 or so Celsius), Mother woke up to hear a whining bark at the kitchen door. There stood a small brown whippet, no coat, shivering uncontrollably. So of course she brought it in, prepared some warm milk, and settled the dog in a warm spot underneath the gas stove beside Nicky, who didn't seem to be concerned one way or another. At breakfast time someone let her out, and she presumably went home. She returned several times, however, and Mother began to tire of the homeless wonder showing up to disturb her rest.

Inquiries round the neighbourhood revealed that the whippet's name was Mitzi and that she belonged immediately back of us on

Glenrose Avenue. Mother spoke to the owners, and apparently Mitzi had a habit of asking "out, please" at bedtime and sometimes showing up either hours later or not at all. She was a dog equivalent of a night person and a real floozie. If she couldn't rouse her people, she crawled under the fence and came to us. What could she have been up to roaming the streets when righteous, well-brought-up dogs were safe in their beds? We always wondered about her and about Nicky's indifference to her. Perhaps she really was a streetwalker, and he clearly did not count her as a friend. He certainly had girlfriends. He and a German shepherd about twice his size used to walk off to the ravine together, and of course there was the confrontation outside Loblaws about his alleged fatherhood.

Mitzi's family apologized for causing us inconvenience and made the fence dogproof. Then one night she showed up at the front door. Dad told her to go home in kind but firm tones, and, although we saw her around in the day, she never came whining to us at night again.

Twice a week, more often in a heat wave, the iceman, with cart and horse, delivered a huge block, one hundred pounds, of ice that he carried on a leather piece on his shoulder directly to the icebox in the kitchen. Iceboxes all had trays underneath that needed emptying every day. One of the brothers drilled through the floor into the cellar a hole that was so close to a drain that it rendered obsolete the boys' daily task. Parents and the iceman strictly forbade it, but on a hot day it was fun to climb up the back of the cart and take a shard of ice to suck, after one wiped off the sawdust, of course. The adults' opposition enhanced this surreptitious pleasure.

Gradually, one by one, horses disappeared from the street, giving way to noisy motor vehicles. It was only when they had all departed that we realized how much we missed the friendly, rhythmic clop, clop of their hooves. I wondered where the sparrows would seek their food. Earlier I had said how disgusting the birds were, pecking at the horse's waste. Mother had corrected me: they were finding undigested seeds, a perfectly natural thing for them to do, and there was nothing disgusting about it.

One horse remained on duty, however, for the mounted policeman who patrolled Moore Park, including Inglewood Drive, every day except Sunday. Horse and rider showed up about three o'clock in the afternoon, and the horse halted in front of 139. Despite a pat on the neck from the officer, he wasn't going to move until one of us came out with a carrot. Pat was our principal horse lover, so it was always his turn, but when he was at school I took over. Mother had shown me what to do: how to place the carrot on the palm of my hand and, after she had lifted me up for him to take it so gently, how to stroke his nose while he munched. She told us that if no one were home, one of the four Lailey girls next door would be sure to take him the treat that he demanded.

Outside the Royal Ontario Museum, on Bloor Street West, a water trough for horses remained in place long after the beautiful creatures had disappeared from Toronto streets – even those of the Misses Mortimer Clark who lived opposite the museum. Their gated mansion – where the Park Hyatt Hotel stands now – had its own stables, and they had gone for an outing in their brougham each afternoon. Whenever, sitting upright and looking like something out of an old *Illustrated News*, they passed Mother, they always bowed to her, as she did in return and bade me do the same. That I had never met the ladies made no difference – Mother had on several occasions, and bow my head slightly I must. One of many musicians from Europe who joined us right after the Second World War told me that he knew that he would like Toronto: it had a horse trough on a main street, which dogs going for a walk used, as well as ring-necked pheasants who sauntered about unconcerned in the museum grounds. Pheasants make such good eating, he said, and nobody bothers them. After the deprivations and hunger of the war years, it was simply remarkable to him.

The Willans weren't the only animal lovers on the block. Mrs Lailey next door devised a lovely present to entertain Terry, their Kerry Blue terrier, his fur dripping down over his eyes, and our Nicky. On very hot days she would collect all her daughters who cared to come – Connie or Joan, and my special friend, Ann – our dogs, and me. We would drive out St Clair Avenue West to where it crosses Weston Road and Keele Street, with the Toronto Stockyards to the south and the Maple Leaf Abattoir to the north.

The smell was palpable. Terry and Nicky, leaning as far out of the car as possible without committing suicide, their forelegs completely out of the windows, were in ecstasy. We all laughed hysterically at their antics. Often we drove home through a flutter of evening newspapers that boys dodging traffic were selling on the street to men in cars. The *Toronto Daily Star* and the pink *Evening Telegram* each cost two cents. Most customers held out change – some of them, the old, large one-cent coins – that the boys took while handing them a paper, and the whole exchange seemed to involve but a single gesture.

Our Nicky was a natural clown. He didn't do tricks for tidbits, but at the request, "Nicky, be funny," he would grab anything lying around – a bone that he was working on, a visitor's glove, a dinner napkin, a raw carrot, a favourite snack. He pranced and danced with the object in his mouth, tossed it in the air, and swivelled and caught it, all to our applause. One evening he flung a bone with such vigour that it sailed across the room and landed on the strings of the Mason & Risch grand piano with a crashing dissonance. He turned around with a "who did that?' look on his face but recovered quickly after a delirious reception. From then on, heaving something with substance towards the piano became the climax of his circus performance. Sometimes he hit it, sometimes not.

Terry Lailey next door had just one trick. His family had trained him to sit in front of the treat giver, place his paws on his or her knees, and bow his head in prayer. At "Amen," he could raise his head and take his treat. Terence Crosthwait, curate of Grace Church On-the-Hill, arrived for tea at the Laileys' sometime in the early 1930s; he asked Terry to say his prayers and then blessed him before he said "Amen." Ann and I thought it a kindly thing to do, but it shocked some older people who thought that a clergyman should not bless a dog.

Each of our dogs experienced a traumatic moment in Dad's study. Over the mantelpiece hung Beethoven's death mask, larger than life or else he had an abnormally large head. Some puppies cowered, a couple barked, for this apparition nonplussed all of them, but since it didn't move or bark back the shock passed in time.

Our home, almost on the corner of Inglewood and Clifton Road, which led south from St Clair to Our Lady of Perpetual Help School, seemed far more crucial to animal lovers than the Humane Society. Even though automobiles moved at speeds laughably slow by today's notion, there were no stop signs. At least four or five times a summer we would hear a hideous crash and would usually see a body on the sidewalk. I'm sure others helped too, but we seemed always to be the household that people used to telephone for an ambulance or a doctor. We contributed a fair number of blankets to cover the injured and never saw them again. When stop signs went up at the crossing, the carnage stopped, and we saved substantially on bed coverings.

Diagonally across from our house was a woods. The brothers used to prowl there, looking for whatever young boys used to find and put in their pockets. One or another of them would tell me that they had found something really good and invite me to put my hand in a pocket for a real prize. I bit every time and plunged my hand in to come up with a wriggling garter snake or a toad, much to my horror. The brothers found this thoroughly amusing.

When a house went up on the lot, it quite spoiled their fun. A great many homes were going up around us until the Depression slowed construction, and they provided us with early-evening entertainment. After the workmen had left, Ann Lailey and I used to inspect the day's progress, lay a few bricks ourselves if the mortar were still soft, and generally clamber about the scaffolding.

PART III

The 1930s

UNIVERSITY OF TORONTO
Royal Toronto Conservatory of Music

A MANUAL
OF
EAR-TRAINING
AND
SIGHT-SINGING
BY
GLADYS WILLAN

A Collection of Exercises and Tests based upon the examination requirements of the Junior, Intermediate and Senior Grades in Sight-Singing, of the Toronto Conservatory of Music.

THE FREDERICK HARRIS MUSIC CO. LIMITED

ENGLAND:
14 BERNERS STREET,
LONDON, W.1

CANADA:
DUNDAS STREET, OAKVILLE,
ONTARIO

CHAPTER EIGHT

Art, Sister Anna, and Current Events

(1930–1935)

In the early days of the Depression, about 1931 or 1932, fine art was beginning to interest me more than music. One day, walking home from St Mildred's – where I started again, but as a daygirl, about 1931 – I passed Mr Tyrrell's bookshop on Yonge Street. One of the windows in the store displayed coloured etchings, mainly European scenes by Nicholas Hornyansky. They were 15 cents each. I felt that urge to acquire. The next day I went in to see Mr Tyrrell and negotiate. My pocket money was ten cents a week, of which five went for church collection, way overdoing tithing, I thought. I asked the owner if I could pay him five cents a week for one of the etchings, and he thought that quite possible. I pondered a bit – the pictures were all rather attractive – and decided on a view of old houses in Amsterdam. Mr Tyrrell started wrapping it up, but I said that I would prefer instead to pick it up in three weeks when I had paid for it, which I did.

When I reached home with my prize, I showed off my etching to Dad, who looked at the signature and said, "That's my girl. Nicky has a few hanging up in the club, and he's trying to give them away." That remark crushed me. I laid the treasure carefully in the bottom of the bottom drawer in my room, where it stayed until I left home.

I still have it, and I still like it, and it's worth considerably more than the purchase price; moreover keeping it flat in the dark for many years has probably prolonged its life.

At St Mildred's, girls who wished to could sit the annual art examinations of Britain's Royal Drawing Society. Sister Una, our art mistress, had studied in England and had made contact with the society for her pupils. The exams, a gruelling three or four hours, always took place on a hot day in June. There was a primary year, and eight grades followed. If you did not pass primary, you could not go on. First-class marks in all eight grades virtually guaranteed admission to the Slade School in London.

I signed up when I was about 12, and three of us did obtain our full school certificates, with first class in all grades. The average age at completion was 18, but we were considerably younger, having completed two or three grades per year. The Slade was out of reach for all of us, however; we were too young, and the possibility of war was looming in the distance.

One afternoon Dad asked me what I had been doing so quietly in my room for hours. I explained that I had two art exams coming up and had to prepare. He inquired, "You really would rather do that than practise the piano, wouldn't you?" I replied, "Yes." "Well then, you don't have to practise the piano if you don't want to." This was a great relief to me, and it pleased me that he understood where my true interests were heading. I really did enjoy listening to music more than performing it.

Everybody had to tighten their belts when the Great Depression hit home. Evelyn Pamphilon had helped my parents to discover 139 Inglewood for us in 1920. As she put it, "It's the big things I can't afford I can do without. I shall not be travelling to Europe this summer. It's the little, everyday things I took for granted that are so annoying to do without." She augmented her piano-teaching income by producing a pamphlet, *What's On,* listing local concerts and recitals as well as dance performances, a first in Toronto. She charged a low fee for a notice and sold *What's On* by subscription. It didn't make her rich, but it helped her manage. The other Toronto pamphlet, *Gossip* – an accurate label – went to subscribers (and a few other people, such as the Willans) weekly by mail.

At St Mary Magdalene's Church, collections became so meager that there was talk of closing down. At a vestry meeting, Dad offered to take a 50-per-cent reduction in what was never a large salary for the duration of the economic slowdown. I don't think that anybody remembered to put it back to normal when things were more flourishing, and Dad never reminded the church of his temporary arrangement. Father Gavitt thought to save a bit of money by extinguishing the seven sanctuary lights in the chancel during the night. The first time he tried it, the policeman making his rounds awakened him about three in the morning. He wanted to know what was wrong, no candles flickering in the church. The rector explained about cutting costs, and the policeman was glad to learn that it was nothing serious. He insisted on paying for candles at night. "I'm a Catholic," he told the rector, "and those lights I can see through the church windows mean so much to me. I get a real sense of peace, something I need in this job." Considering the little pay that policemen received, the gesture must have been a sacrifice for him.

That a Catholic should find comfort in the aura of a Protestant church was a surprise to us. Catholics and Protestants didn't do much socializing in that era, ecumenism had not yet moved to the fore, and sometimes feelings ran high, especially on July 12, at the Orangemen's parade down Yonge Street.

At one time there was an oil painting in the church, a Nativity perhaps, not a masterpiece, but the only artwork there. Somebody entered the church and slashed it. Perhaps it was a fellow Protestant who thought that St Mary's was becoming too high-church, too chummy with Rome, too papist. Repairing the item would have cost money, but it hung in the basement, a reminder, as one of the Sisters of the Church observed, to be tolerant of others' ideas even if you do not agree with them.

To me, if not to some of our Protestant neighbours, St Mildred's College, which the Anglican Sisters of the Church ran, seemed a good place, even during the Depression. My school friends were Protestants of all types or Jews, and we seemed to get along beautifully. Our Protestant neighbours at home, except the Laileys and a few others, figured that I was a Catholic, and their children would not play with me. One neighbour treated Mother and me with disdain, waving her hand around her face and muttering something about the pope's salute, whatever that meant. The Catholics certainly would not play with me, for I was not one of them. The best thing to do was to ignore them too and follow Mother's advice – since everybody doesn't love everybody else, just be with the people who do like you and forget the rest.

A cello entered my life too after I gave up piano for fine art. Mother found me one, badly used and forsaken, and took it to Bill Haenhel, the master caretaker of all string instruments. Of course, it arrived at home in pristine form, my Christmas present from Dad. With both parents being such wholehearted and complete musicians, it simply didn't cross their minds that we lesser mortals need lessons to play these things.

I learned by trial and error where to find the notes – 'fingering,' they call it. Mother oversaw the handling of the bow, but it was harder to play than a piano, which at least had notes in black and white. I took myself off to the attic with a copy of a Brahms violin sonata that Mother and Isabel Auden, who lived around the corner, used to play together. I liked the tune, so simply played it an octave lower and whacked away, very slowly. It took me several weeks to figure out three or four bars, so I gave it up. Practically every musician who visited 139 and possibly heard the mournful noise from the attic advised me not to use Leo Smith's brand of resin.

In the meantime, Bunny had acquired a saxophone and, being Bunny, painted it white, with gold ornaments. He managed to learn a few current tunes on it and then took it apart piece by piece. A few months later he brought home a clarinet, a beautiful thing in the hands of a good player. He coaxed some atrocious sounds out of it, and a clarinet's sound carries well. Various parties asked him to tone it down, and pretty soon it went silent. He did not paint it and only partly dismembered it.

Saturday afternoon in opera season was sacred to the radio performances from the old Metropolitan Opera in New York with the growling, very distinctive voice of Mrs August Belmont urging us all to invest in the Met-tro-pol-itan Op-era. This was in the worst of the Depression and before Texaco began to pick up the tab. Years later I was at the 'Met' on 34th Street and after a performance stood beside a tiny woman, erect, submerged in furs, as I hailed a cab and she summoned the doorman to open her limousine door. That voice! It was Mrs Belmont; and the doorman told me that she was well into her 90s. She had been a singer herself at the Met before her marriage, and her diction was still as clear, compelling, and distinctive as I remembered it. That voice was as much a part of Saturday afternoon as the nasal Milton J. Cross describing the great gold curtains coming slowly down. You had the impression that all of us opera lovers across North America were letting out a deep breath of satisfaction at another stellar performance and at the stars whom we had heard.

We had our own connection to those Saturday afternoons. Over at St Clair and Yonge was a delicatessen, Feinsod's. A radio in the shop was always on at the Met performances. Woe betide the nincompoop who interrupted an aria to talk about potato salad. If it were a Puccini opera, Mrs Feinsod simply ignored the customer altogether. She was in some way a relative of the composer's, and to interrupt a note of his was sheer blasphemy. You waited for the applause and just pointed to what you wanted. Feinsod's also sold a three-decker little cake interlaced with cream and pistachios; I have seen its twin only in a shop in Nice. For us it was a birthday treat.

Many European musicians, having fled Russia or Germany in the Great War, arrived in Britain, where they found stiff competition from many brilliant performers. Some kept on going until they reached Canada, where they made tremendous contributions both as teachers and as performers. Alexander Chuhaldin was one, arriving in Toronto in 1927 with a solid reputation from a tour in Asia, Australia, and New Zealand. For quite a while, he regularly conducted radio performances for the Canadian Broadcasting Corporation (CBC). When he reached Toronto he came to pay his respects to Dad and Mother. As he left, he took Mother's hand and kissed it, and then to my horror he did the same to me. After he had gone, I wanted to wash my hand. Mother made it very clear to me that he had come from eastern Europe – his birthplace was in the Crimea – and that kissing a lady's hand was a mark of respect that I was to accept as such without fuss. European manners were easier for Mother than New World customs such as a guest of honour's seemingly serving as maid at a tea party.

Chuhaldin became conductor of the Cleveland Symphony and took a mediocre orchestra to the highest standards, according to the critics. At one point Toronto and Cleveland exchanged conductors for a concert. The Cleveland players found Sir Ernest MacMillan's tempi slow and dubbed him 'Lord Largo.'

My life at St Mildred's changed abruptly with the arrival of a new headmistress. Sister Anna was a graduate of Radcliffe College, the women's offshoot of Harvard, when the latter was a male preserve. She had begun a brilliant career as a specialist in international law and then suddenly dropped it and joined the Sisters of the Church. She knew nothing about running a girl's school, so she consulted Dr William Blatz, head of Child Study at the University of Toronto, well known for his innovative ideas. In a day of male dominance in every field, Sister Anna wanted to make us independent thinkers.

Sister Anna established a system of houses and named them Brant, Cartier, and Grenfell, each with prefects – senior students who monitored young ones. At her request, Dad wrote the school song, *Jubilate Deo*. She also invited persons of interest to come and address the whole school from time to time. Sir Wilfred Grenfell, the physician who fitted out hospital ships for fishermen and established hospitals and other services in Labrador, spoke to us about his Grenfell Mission and gave us an appreciation for the high artistic level of the crafts created. The girls in Grenfell House at St Mildred's felt privileged. We in Brant House and the girls in Cartier House were unable to welcome our namesakes.

Another day an actress, a friend of Marjorie Pickthall's, a greatly overlooked Canadian poet who had attended St Mildred's in its early years, read her poems to us. It was the first time that I had heard someone read poetry out loud without a musical background, and it was magical.

Monday morning at St Mildred's opened with Current Events. Each of us had to prepare for it by clipping each weekday what we thought the most important news event from the daily paper. Sister Anna taught us to read a newspaper by concentrating on the front page – right-hand side, then left – and next turning to the editorial page to see what the editors had thought about the preceding day's news. Then we went to page 2, which presented interesting news not of the first importance.

Each Monday morning we took our clippings to school, discussed our findings, and then counted up the selections to find out what the majority decided. You had to be ready to defend your choice if it did not agree with the majority. We made a chart on the board, tallied everybody's choices, and determined each day's winning and most significant choice. Each week we voted on that week's most important development. It was a lively way to start a Monday, with the barely-in-their-teens crowd arguing with conviction about world events.

Some of us were subscribers to an English publication, Arthur Mee's *Children's Newspaper,* which concentrated on major international events such as Britain's going off the gold standard in 1931. An editorial by Mee made the change seem reasonable, even though Toronto papers were crying doom. It helped us to round out our choices.

Thanks to Sister Anna's dicta, our class had turned into a covey of free thinkers. A younger member of the staff made a remark about Ethiopia's being a backward place and Mussolini's merely giving it civilization by invading it in 1934. Our class rose together in horror, and each of us expounded on the evils of fascism and Mussolini's unwarranted invasion. We called it a land grab and mentioned the incipient danger of Germany and Italy's allying for another war.

A man arrived another day to tell us about a famine in India and encouraged us to give money to buy wheat to send to the starving people. He asked for a show of hands for volunteers. I put up my hand, but not as a volunteer. I said that my pocket money was ten cents a week. I would tithe if the Nizam of Hyderabad, reportedly the richest man in the world, would do likewise. I had stamps of the Nizam in a jewel-encrusted turban that would have paid for food for many people. The talk on saving starving Indians ended abruptly.

One history class a week centred on 'The Dark Ages,' which era had that name, Sister Anna observed, only because we did not know much about it. Her contention was that the period 500–1000 AD established much of the thinking and culture of the modern world. We ploughed through it century by century, having to look up facts and figures in some unlikely sources, and gained a respect for cultures other than western European.

Sister Anna was keen for us to undertake independent research for our classes and on making sure that whatever resource we used was reliable, or relatively so. In a Canadian history class, she encouraged our teacher, Miss Harrington, whom we all adored, to take us out into the Ontario Legislative Building to observe our representatives in action from the visitors' gallery. The school chose a date for our crocodile walk to Queen's Park. My particular friend, Peggy Tucker, and I couldn't make it on that day. We were working on a project for the school bazaar – a puppet theatre to be a feature involving the whole class. The two of us were the architects, and we had enlisted Peggy's brother Frank to help us nail the thing together that afternoon.

We had to promise to go to Queen's Park on our own, and we did. It impressed us too, but not in the same way that it did the others in the class. For them it was a bit solemn, dignified, almost boring. On our day, Liberal Premier Mitchell Hepburn started shouting at the leader of the opposition, former Conservative premier George Henry. The two politicians became rather hot under their respective collars. Henry yelled at Hepburn, calling him "a damned onion grower." Failing to bring order to the chaos, the Speaker absented himself from the House, with the pages trailing.

Then the fun really began. We even learned some new swear words. Our elected representatives behaved like a bunch of little boys fighting over something unimportant in a schoolyard – a delightful afternoon's entertainment. Our report duly joined the other, for, as Miss Harrington pointed out, looking at more than one side of an event was a helpful way to understand the whole process.

CHAPTER NINE

Fascinating Friends and a Wider World
(1932–1935)

I was alone in the house at 139 one afternoon after school when the phone rang. A woman's voice asked to speak to Miss Willan. I couldn't imagine who Miss Willan was. I asked her please to hold the line. In bewilderment and walking round and round the living-room, I suddenly realized that this woman referred to 12-year-old me as Miss Willan. What a surprise! I went back to the phone more or less in shock and managed to tell the caller that Miss Willan was speaking! It was Mrs Cody, wife of the new university president. I certainly knew Canon Cody, but I had never met his spouse. She was inviting me to assist at a reception at the Royal Ontario Museum, which was an adjunct of the university in those days. I managed to say that it would be an honour for me.

At the reception, I worked together with Monica Allcott – a friend of mine from St Mildred's College whose father was also on the university staff, in architecture, I think. We carried coffee cups on one tray and cream and sugar on another around to guests, all university staff types. Poliomyelitis had paralysed Monica's left arm, so she rested the cream-and-sugar tray on her useless left arm. I carried the coffee-cup tray with one hand and poured the cream with the other. We really had not known each other well, but we soon made a great team for Mrs Cody's receptions.

Many faculty members rather dreaded those evenings. Dad never went: the events took place on Fridays, so he had an excuse, Friday being for choir practice. At one of the receptions, our friend and neighbour Dr Harold Ball ('Uncle Harold' to me), who was professor of histology, found Mother, thoroughly bored, gazing at the fish in the aquarium that used to overlook the rotunda. "Contemplating suicide by drowning, are we?" asked the physician. Mother threw back her head and laughed so hard that she nearly capsized into the tank. "How typical of Harold to get some fun out of a dull moment," she said next morning.

Uncle Harold had served with the Canadian Army Medical Corps in France during the Great War. He once told me that he was afraid of only three things – women, hell, and guns, and in that order. People said of him that he had only to walk into a patient's room and recovery started immediately. He told me one day about a little trick that he had played at a cocktail party. Apparently a man who often cadged free medical advice, before the days of socialized medicine, approached him and started off telling him about his ailments. Uncle Harold listened in his most professional way and then told the man that he thought that he might prescribe something that would help. "And I happen to have my prescription pad with me," he said to the freeloader, telling me the story with a wonderful smirk on his face. He told the man not to read it now, but to take it home and read it then, otherwise everyone would want advice, and this was a party. "What did you write on that pad?" I asked. "Very sound advice," he said, grinning. "I wrote, 'Walk to work.'"

Uncle Harold and his wife, Mandy, were both superb actors. He had a ringing bass voice and in some radio CBC production played the voice of God. The director had an inspired idea. Uncle Harold would declaim at the top of the staircase in the old Coverley House, home to the CBC, on Jarvis Street, with the microphone down on the first floor. The rehearsal was splendid, God seemingly intoning from the top of a high mountain. The program was live on air, and as God was uttering an injunction about doom or whatever, some witless wonder flushed a toilet on the second floor. Uncle Harold was positively giggling when he told us about the effect that had on everyone, from the producer on down. "I felt I was condemning Noah as well," he said.

Uncle Harold was a stickler for cleanliness. He made his house calls carrying a supply of freshly ironed linen handkerchiefs. Before anything else, he washed his hands and dried them on one of the hankies, repeating the action on another before he left the house. Mrs Ball washed and ironed many handkerchiefs. She was also on a daily radio serial at CFRB, Monday to Friday at noon. It was part of a farm news program, which offered the market price of eggs, meat, and poultry and news of interest to farmers.

One sloppy, slushy February morning Uncle Harold drove her downtown to CFRB on University Avenue. On the way she spied a young woman standing on the corner of Bay and Bloor streets waiting for a streetcar with a baby in her arms. Full of compassion, she begged her husband to give the two a lift. The doctor took a good look at the woman and demurred. Aunt Mandy insisted. "Very well," said Uncle Harold. "Hop in, Madam, and close the door. I presume you are on your way to the Hospital for Sick Children. I will drive you there." "Oh, thank you," the young woman said. "Yes, we go to Sick Kids. Me and baby got syphilix!" Mandy froze. After mother and child left the car, she turned on Uncle Harold. "You knew she was sick, didn't you?" He just smiled when he told me about it. "Mandy spent all afternoon scrubbing out the back seat with Javex."

A group of madcap types – Dad, Uncle Harold Ball, and many Arts and Letters members – formed a club of sorts that they called Birds of a Feather. Membership was by invitation only. The fellows were rather secretive about their doings; innocent fun seemed to be their chief motive, but they had an initiation ceremony. Apparently they gave the new member a tankard of beer, which he had to finish without a pause for breath. The tankard had a glass bottom, and some prankster had glued a small ceramic frog to the bottom. If you could keep your dinner down, you were in.

Each member had a secret name of a bird. Uncle Harold was the Capon. Well over six feet tall and heavily built, he and his wife had no children, hence the name. I never have learned Dad's avian namesake – a musical singer, I hope. New Year's Eve parties were the only events that wives could attend and took place in the penthouse of the Sampson, Matthews building on Yonge Street – both Mr Matthews and Mr Sampson were founding members. Their lithography firm was famous for the high quality of its colour prints of paintings, its photographic inventions, and its illustrious staff members.

One of Mother's school chums was Amice Calverley, the world's leading woman Egyptologist, who was working in Abydos under the Rockefeller Foundation. She used to drop in from time to time for tea or for lunch. She and Mother used to recall gleefully Miss somebody or other's Academy for the Daughters of Gentlemen. Each morning they had to march around the drill hall with a wand tucked into their elbows behind their backs. This was to give them straight backs and a ladylike carriage, as though they had been riding sidesaddle all their lives. At the same time they had to keep repeating "prunes and prisms" without moving their jaws to give them the proper British upper-crust lockjaw speech. It didn't work on Mother, thank goodness.

In 1932, Mother rounded up a few other Academy survivors for a luncheon. This was to be more formal than her usual meetings with Amice. Everything was going splendidly until Mother's kitchen help, Mrs Fogarty, decided to jazz up the dessert, something chilled and white in glass cups. She looked around the kitchen and found the cayenne, just about Dad's favourite spice, which he lavished on everything from radishes to curried lamb. Mrs Fogarty wasn't great at reading labels, so apparently dessert was a bit of a surprise, with a liberal sprinkling of something red for looks. General laughter ensued, until Amice fell off her chair in a dead faint. The ladies hovered around with water and general loosening of collar and belt, but they could not bring her round.

Mother telephoned Dad, who immediately called his medical pals on the university staff, Uncle Harold Ball and others. The word shot around like lightning apparently: Nell's pal the Egyptologist is unconscious, and they can't revive her. Dr Burton from the Physics Department arrived at 139 with the medics. An electron microscope, his newest toy, which I believe he had helped develop, was uppermost in his mind.

The group managed to move the patient onto a couch in the living-room, and Dr Burton had the inspired idea of taking a culture from the inside of her nose. He rushed back to his microscope and identified viruses, the sort that would inhabit a cavern closed for centuries, the lowest order in a food chain that had bats at the top. There had been other instances in which workers in King Tut's tomb suddenly lost consciousness as the viruses worked their way up through the sinuses, giving rise to a popular myth about the tomb's curse. Abydos is not far from the tomb, and the latest victim had spent years in poorly ventilated conditions.

She recovered, but in the days before antibiotics or even sulfa drugs bed rest was the usual prescription. Accordingly we moved her into Mother's bedroom, where she spent several weeks recovering her strength. Each day a contingent from the medical faculty showed up to mark progress and to chat with our distinguished visitor. Each day after school I headed home in a hurry for the foot of her bed, and we gossiped.

She told me of her adventures as a guest on various yachts in the Mediterranean, the first time that I had heard someone refer to it as 'the Med.' Apparently the rich and bored made a habit of inviting what we now call 'achievers' to be their guests. "Too limp-headed to keep each other amused," was Amice Calverley's comment. She recounted juicy tales about King Carol of Romania and Magda

Lupescu, the rather luscious redhead whom he preferred. I gathered that our guest didn't think much of either of them. The Prince of Wales was often on board with someone else's wife – all heady stuff to a 12-year-old. Many people assumed that the Rockefeller Foundation encouraged the Egyptologists to accept these invitations, probably in the hope of raising interest in their findings and attracting funds from the wealthy.

Amice Calverley told me about the time when her brother visited her in Egypt. A *fellah* acting more or less as his batman received a bite from a poisonous snake. Her brother, a decorated major from the Great War, at once sucked the poison out of the man's heel, and he lived. Then the Calverleys found out that, since the man was a Muslim and the major had interfered with the natural turn of events, he was now responsible for the patient as long as he lived. I have forgotten how the matter eventually sorted itself out, but Major Calverley returned to England without him and later settled in Canada.

At the conclusion of the preceding season, springtime before it became too unbearably hot for field work, the archaeologists at Abydos had decided to hold a windup party, and what better venue than King Tut's tomb? As my new friend told me, "Some wag hung a sign over the entrance, 'Tut and come in.'" She wrote a little poem about Abydos and talked Dad into setting it to music for her. One evening our fascinating guest was able to go downstairs briefly, and my parents had invited some friends of hers to hear the *Abydos Air*. Dr Homer Thompson from the university, a Greek and Roman authority, brought his wife, who sang it, to everyone's pleasure. Later I studied Greek and Roman art at the university under him, and shortly thereafter he left for Harvard. His slant on history was not nearly as entertaining as our guest's. Her chats on the goings-on of the pharaohs were much more entertaining. The *Abydos Air* finally appeared in print in 1957, for some special event, I think.

After our star boarder had recovered sufficiently to be up and about, she decided to give Mother some Egyptian cooking lessons.

Egyptians cook rice, she told us, by heating it in a pan with a little oil and just enough water for it to absorb – a natural custom where water is scarce. We tried it and adopted it.

Another day it was a chocolate concoction that Dad labelled 'Mesopotamia Mud.' The ingredients are ½ pound of bitter or plain chocolate; 2 tablespoons of milk; ¼ pound of ground almonds (or matzo flour or farina meal); 6 tablespoons of sugar; 6 eggs, separated; butter and flour; and castor sugar to decorate. Melt the chocolate with the milk in a double boiler. Mix the chocolate with ground almonds, sugar, and egg yolks. Beat the mixture well and pour it into a buttered and floured cake tin, a spring-form pan. Bake this in a pre-heated oven at 375 degrees Fahrenheit for 45 minutes–1 hour. When the cake is cool, turn it out and sprinkle it with sugar.

At the outbreak of war in 1939, many people sent their children out of London and into homes with strangers in the country. Amice turned a pigsty on a property that she had in the English countryside into what she envisioned as a home for several young evacuees. She completely overhauled it, at least to her standards. She wrote to Mother about ordering various things for the children; two dozen potties was one item. Mother laughed uproariously all the way through that letter. Her correspondent had never married, and her ideas about children's needs were certainly original.

The inspection board sensibly turned her offer down flat, which incensed her. Here she had spent a great deal of money renovating her pigsty, children needed accommodation, and what was she going to do with it? "So like Amice," Mother said. After all, the Egyptologist had been living frugally, managing without plumbing as well as avoiding the odd snake. Mother figured that she had just not imagined what sort of shelter small children would require, let alone their care and emotional needs. Besides, how would she have coped with a clutter of lively, noisy, probably mischievous little people anyway? "Thank goodness, the inspection people turned down that crack-brained idea," said Dad.

One day early in several springs, Dad and Mother departed for a festival, probably the opening or reopening of another grand railway hotel. On at least two of these occasions they deposited me with Lina and Elsie Adamson for a few days. Lina was a violin teacher at the conservatory, and Elsie kept house – and what a fascinating place! Originally the coach house of a large property on Woodlawn Avenue, it had a living-room two storeys high, with bedrooms opening onto a balcony overlooking the living-room.

Their mother, Bertha Drechsler Adamson, had been an orchestra conductor in Vienna. There was a wonderful photograph of her, beautiful, upright, and corseted, feminine in her fashionable black gown ornamented with black jet stones, her conducting stick in one hand. To think that a woman could conduct an orchestra, and in Vienna, was heady stuff, and not affecting a semi-masculine black coat and constricting white bow tie.

Elsie bred Pekinese, lovable, demanding Chinese princesses, and cooked the way her Austrian mother had taught her. Each evening, Lina and Elsie played together, with Elsie at their large, square Beckstein piano like Mother's. Lina produced a couple of her young violin students about my age, and Elsie did what she could with me at the piano, but unfortunately the musical evenings of the young did not amount to much.

Elsie loved to cook, and I enjoyed sitting in her kitchen watching her bake things such as Schubertkache and strudel. Those alert little Pekinese, with their big, beady eyes, surrounded her. I would listen as she reminisced about the tales that her Mother had told her of life in Austria and of conducting symphony concerts. For me, it was like having a completely different life. It was a feminist existence so unlike my brother-dominated life at home, and it provided a lovely respite.

My father was always ready to help a fellow musician. He had a call one afternoon in those Depression years from a young graduate of the conservatory, a cellist. In great distress, she sobbed out her story to him. She had played in Toronto and not received any pay, not a highly unusual state of affairs. As a member of the Toronto Musicians Association, an affiliate of the American Federation of Musicians, or AFM, she started the grievance procedure. She had finally learned that her hearing would be in Barrie. She had no car, no money for bus travel. She was loath to spend a whole day on what might be a wild goose chase, so she turned to Dad for advice.

It was just the sort of thing that he would take on. He called the local boss of the union and blasted him in no uncertain terms. Uncle Harold Ball always said that Dad could keep on going for 15 minutes without repeating himself and without using profanities, and I believe that this time he did that, and maybe a little more. There was quite a bit of shouting back and forth. However, in a couple of weeks the young cellist telephoned to thank him. The union had shifted the grievance hearing to Toronto, and the decision forced the producer to pay her the money as per terms of her contract. The union people were always after Dad to join, but he really had no advantage in doing so.

Each June, Dad, Mother, and I made a ritual pilgrimage to the farm of their publisher, Frederick Harris, just outside Oakville. We took the Lakeshore bus, and our hosts' chauffeur, Collier, met us and drove us to the farm. It was a business trip for Dad. He and Harris talked about the forthcoming Frederick Harris Music Publishers catalogue – what he wanted from Dad and what my father planned to write for him. The morning and evening were for pleasure.

One time Mr Harris showed me the farm. Mother, Mrs Harris, their niece Bea Harrison, and Dad left us for coffee and chitchat. Mr Harris and I went calling on Sally, his sow, to whom he had a particular attachment. I thought that enormous Sally, with her bright, knowing eyes, was the best thing on the farm. She smelled a bit, but not much. She kept herself and her piglets remarkably clean. Mr Harris told me that pigs want to be clean: they roll about in the mud because they are trying to cool off. Sally was a perfect mother, training her piglets swiftly, and they obeyed her. According to Mr Harris, pigs are the most intelligent animals on any farm. Sally seemed to acknowledge the compliment with a great snort of appreciation.

Then I entertained myself until a maid called me to lunch. One year I took along my new oil paints and canvas. The farm had a pretty setting on rolling ground with big trees. I soon found a view for a picture and started in. There were some cows in the field, but we paid each other no mind. The maid found me, a little put out that she had had to walk so far. I left my paints in a tidy condition and followed her. I figured that I might never find my way back to my view if I took the paints with me.

After lunch, Dad and Mr Harris turned to business, the women retired to nap before teatime, and I went back, only to find those nosy cows eating my paints and enjoying the turpentine. In response to my annoyance at the presumption of those animals, Mr Harris said that even though cows weren't long on intelligence they were curious. There was a certain amount of panic on the herdsman's part. He thought that the paints might contaminate the milk and make it unsuitable for market. I pointed out that what they had eaten was the earth colours, umbers and ochres, and turpentine was good for people. He didn't believe this young person, but the vet supported me.

I knew that 'turps' was safe for the cows. Mother used as a remedy 'Dutch drops,' almost entirely turpentine. It was an old-country remedy, which a monk in the Netherlands developed several centuries ago. It came in a little box with directions in many languages. It always sold for very little money on the orders of the monastery, so that even the poorest of the poor could afford it. It seemed to be almost a panacaea, but the Harrises encouraged me to leave my paints at home the next time.

Tea was a ladies' affair. Eventually dinner arrived when the sun was almost setting. This was June, candles on the table provided light, and it was past my bedtime. The Harrises' knives and forks were so heavy that I had trouble handling them, but the best part of the day was still to come.

We six gathered around the grand piano, and Dad played for Mrs Harris, who knew every song that anyone ever sang in London's music halls, turn-of-the-century vintage. My parents noticed a certain authenticity in the way that she performed and later told me that they were pretty sure that she had been a music-hall performer. Mr Harris beamed his approval at his wife's performance. My memory of the lyrics is that they were mostly complete nonsense – along the lines of "I haven't had an egg since Easter and now it's half past three!" It was probably just as well that I didn't understand most of the words. Some were of the sort that made the outing something to which 'one didn't take one's maiden aunt.'

With a speed limit of 15 miles an hour, we had a long and sleepy bus ride home from Oakville, but a day with the Harrises was worth it. For a week or so, Dad and Mother reminisced happily about the evening, Mrs Harris's renditions, and places in London, their old haunts. Sometimes they bickered about a street's location and about its name or where it led. That outing to the publisher's home took them back to their young days.

Musicians around town never really understood how the music-publishing company actually worked with a gentleman farmer in Canada in charge and with a London business address. Mother told me that she thought that it had to do with taxes, something that Mr Harris did his best to avoid. The Harrises spent winters somewhere warm; Majorca was a favourite spot.

They gave their composers interesting presents, sometimes rather valuable. A racehorse arrived for Lady MacMillan, to her surprise, but the beast never won anything. Mother received a dessert set of Rosenthal – cream porcelain, octagonal, with borders of 24-carat gold over an inch wide in a rather Florentine type of decoration. These dishes do not go in a dishwasher. Mr Harris presented me with a necklace of Majorcan pearls for my 16th birthday and, on my engagement in 1941, with a magnificent linen tablecloth, larger than any table that I have ever owned, of intricate cut-thread work, also from Majorca I thought, though perhaps Irish. It was always just too great a work of art to run the risk of food or wine stains. It is now safe in Toronto's Textile Museum.

Mr Harris's chief handyman, chauffeur, and general factotum, Reginald Collier, whom he had brought from England as a young man, always addressed me as "Miss Mary," and I called him "Collier," which seemed appropriate for that sort of milieu. When Mr Harris died in 1945, he left his firm to Collier. I became "Mary" and addressed him as "Mr Collier" – an interesting change I thought, which didn't really alter our relationship one bit.

As we saw above, highway speed limits were lower in the 1930s – 15 or 20 miles an hour, which suited roads, tires, and everything underneath the hood. My friend Barbara McLaughlin told me of riding in the rumble seat of her parents' car as they drove to their summer place in Muskoka at a time when the speed limit was 15 miles an hour. The auto must have hit a boulder or a hole in the highway and bounced, throwing 'Hippo' (her nickname) right out of the rumble seat. She landed on the highway, picked herself up, and wandered over to the side of the road. She figured that her parents would miss her eventually and return to pick her up and that in the meantime she might as well pick a bunch of wild flowers for her mother. The McLaughlins did not realize that she was missing for many a mile. Barbara was always calm and patient.

Dora Mavor Moore produced Christmas pageants that played in churches around town and as far outside the city as a bus could carry us, the cast, without our staying overnight ('runouts'). With long blonde hair, again I was the angel, no wig necessary, either taking good news to shepherds or standing over the stable in the closing scene. One year I had to climb from a chair to a table, from there find the step-ladder, make my way up to the top, and then stand while stretching out my arms – all of this in a blackout. When Mrs Moore wanted a dramatic effect, she told us to do it, and we did it, not even asking head or feet first.

At one church, rather a small one, I missed the chair, somehow ended up on the chancel rail, could not find a table or step-ladder, and had to back up and start again. This situation of course messed up the count that Fran on the spotlight and I had worked through in rehearsal. So when I was half-way up the ladder, in the ungainly posture of rear end sticking far out, Fran turned on the spot and then turned it off fast. After giving me a few counts, he turned it back on, and all was well that ended well. I still don't know how anyone could do that monkey climb in pitch dark and silence and then stand on the very top, but Mrs Moore's word was law.

One Easter, Mrs Moore produced *Everyman*, and we did runouts east and west of Toronto, as well as at several venues in town. One of the best was in Hamilton, at a very large Presbyterian church, St Paul's on James Street South, I think. The cast arrived in a bus, and we did our run-through, entrances coming from under the choir stalls around the back of the chancel, a great effect.

The women of the church fed us an evening meal of cold roast pork, scalloped potatoes, and cole slaw. Mavor Moore sat way up at one end of a long table, and I at the end of another – *Everyman* has a large cast. When one of the hostesses bent over me and asked so considerately if I wished another helping of meat, Mavor hooted out, "Hey, Willansky, you can't eat that. That's PORK." Our hostess froze and moved back. Whether serving pork to a Jew or serving a Jew in her Christian church horrified her I have never figured out, but many people were anti-semitic back then. I thought that Mavor was as usual hilarious, and so did the rest of the cast, which probably helped to confuse the good Calvinist women.

We had more than *Everyman* that night, an extra performance in the wings, as it were. The minister's brother was a bit of an over-imbiber. That evening he chose to wander into the church by a back door. He took quite a fancy to one of the seven deadly sins, Helen German, a sister of Isobel Auden's, a tiny, very attractive blonde in a suitably fetching costume. We had to remove him by fair means or foul and without sound, no raining on Mavor's parade out on stage, where he was doing a very creditable job of Everyman.

Murray Paulin played Confessor in a sort of white bishop's costume; Patrick Watson was the devil in the usual black-and-red tights, cloak, and horns. Those two cooked up a mime performance and cast me, already in costume to play the angel who goes on stage at the very end, taking care of Everyman. Patrick prodded the drunk with his trident, with Murray waving an outsized cross and me flapping big wings, and we eased our victim out of the church. He was too surprised to make a sound, thank goodness. When we last saw him, he was running down the middle of James Street, his feet not quite reaching the ground. We held our sides as we nearly convulsed at our successful drama.

Another *Everyman* took place in St Paul's Church on Avenue Road in Toronto, which had beautiful art-deco frescoes by Gustav Hahn before it burned to the ground. Again we arrived in a bus with no time to spare and only one big room to change into costume. Without a word, we each grabbed our own hangers and headed for a spot at the side of the room. Most of us had to strip almost to the buff to climb into the medieval costumes. We didn't think anything of it – the play and being ready were the only things on our minds. Something happened that we didn't notice and heard about only later from Mel Breen, a cast member, whose family belonged to the church. Apparently an elder of St Paul's opened the door and saw about 20 young people, boys and girls, all in a state of undress and paying no attention to each other. He claimed that the sight did not shock, only surprised him.

At one point in the 1930s Dora Mavor Moore shared premises with Mel Keay the costume designer. When I wasn't in a class, I was working under Mel. He would hand me plain stomachers and boxes of baubles and shiny bits, needle and thread, sometimes glue, and I made designs to grace those youngsters taking the part of Elizabethan ladies – much more fun than practising piano. Mel had an incredible gift; he could match any colour from memory. There are so many variations of a bluish-green colour for instance, but he could prowl through the fabric department at Eaton's or Simpson's and swoop onto some remnant that was an exact match for a piece of fabric back in the studio. It was a source of wonder to us all. Occasionally a bunch of us teenagers would spend a Saturday evening working on costumes for one of Mrs Moore's productions or something for which Mel was wardrobe master. We would be kidding each other, having a great time together. It beat spending our allowance on a movie.

In the early 1930s it took real courage and unwarranted faith for a couple to marry, particularly in a profession like music, without a regular pay cheque every two weeks. When Dad told Mother that Harold Sumberg, leader of the second-violin section of the Toronto Symphony Orchestra, had wed, Mother said at once that we must have a party for him and his bride. It was June, so the lilac bushes were in full bloom – no need to buy flowers. Invitations went to the entire orchestra, and Mother started cooking up a storm. Bringing instruments was a foregone solution to entertainment, and our garden could hold orchestra members, friends, and relatives. Harold was very popular, and with so much dreariness all around the prospect of a party cheered everyone.

It was a lively event, light-hearted and brimming with good cheer. I was big enough to help Mother with the baking, but I watched the goings-on from her bedroom window when I was supposed to be in bed. There were candles in the garden, speeches, all kinds of music. In short, the neighbours knew that we were giving a party. Eating al fresco was not common in Toronto back then, although our family did it all the time from spring to autumn.

The wedding party nonplussed our neighbours. So many of our habits were at variance with the norm of the nine-to-five crowd. Garden parties usually took place in the afternoon. 'WASPs' and even Catholics would be acceptable at such an event – but such a noisy crowd, everyone making music, and some of them, including the bridegroom, Jewish? What is the neighbourhood coming to? We stared them all down on that occasion and continued in our unorthodox ways. We later found out that many liked the fact that we had broken some kind of barrier.

One year – probably 1933 or 1934 – when Dad was going to be away teaching all summer, Mary Hamilton, founder and director of the Margaret Eaton School of physical fitness, as well as founder and director of Camp Tanamakoon in Algonquin Park, approached Mother and Dora Mavor Moore. She wanted them to take on drama and music programs at the camp for July and August. The two friends talked it over. Fran Moore had fractured his leg, and his mother wasn't going to leave him in town; what Mavor and Pete did, I don't know. Mother had me on her hands, so all four of us went to Tanamakoon. Poor Fran kept out of sight as much as possible, with so many young females around, but he was a tremendous help backstage as always. I became a camper.

Mother and Mrs Moore's friend at the Heliconian Club, Freda Stark, a good and thoroughly overlooked painter, was having a thin time, as did most artists in the 1930s. Mother suggested that the camp would benefit from outdoor sketching sessions, and Mary Hamilton agreed. Miss Stark was a splendid teacher and became very popular with the campers. Our best efforts went up on the bulletin board, and we all became very competitive about her choices for display.

Miss Hamilton had strict ideas on behaviour. Campers whom she invited to her cabin for a rundown on their shortcomings could take note as they left. She had placed a quatrain inked in birch bark over the top of the door lintel: "The gum chewing girl and the cud chewing cow / Are somewhat alike yet different somehow. / What is the difference? Oh, yes I know now, / It's the thoughtful smile on the face of the cow."

In the 1930s Dad was home more frequently during the week, because the Depression meant fewer musical performances. At dinner one evening in 1933 he told Mother about Harold Sumberg and a couple of other string players from the Toronto Symphony Orchestra who had come to see him that afternoon at the conservatory. They were in great distress. The orchestra had cancelled some of its concerts for the end of the season, and the men were bitter. They told Dad that nearly all of them would have no way to pay their rent. Conductor Ernest MacMillan was off examining for the Royal College of Music, London, leaving them high and dry and understandably angry. Dad had a broad shoulder, and they called on him for advice. He was sympathetic of course but unsure how he could help.

At dinner that evening, Mother proffered a solution: "Why couldn't we have concerts? Something like Sir Henry Wood's Promenade Concerts at the Royal Albert Hall in London." Ideas often flew the length of the table thick and fast; my parents would toss some out and reserve others for more thought and discussion. This particular evening we had a long and lively dinner, the initial planning of a series that would eventually become the Promenade Symphony Concerts. By the end of the meal, Dad was to contact the orchestra's concertmaster to ask him to sound out the members.

Both parents were thinking. Soon Mother proposed talking to Col. R.Y. Eaton about the availability of the auditorium in Eaton's College Street store. It was dark all summer; perhaps he could help. Dad was mulling over a possible program or two. Time was short. There would have to be rehearsals, perhaps a soloist. The choice of dates led to advertising and sale of tickets. "Ticket prices must be kept as low as possible, like the Proms in London, so that anybody with any kind of employment could afford it," was Mother's pronouncement. Somehow volunteers showed up. The newspapers created good publicity. 'Feel good' stories about cheap symphony music, something new for Toronto, were a bit of a heart-warmer in the Depression.

Everything was proceeding smoothly, too smoothly. The musicians wanted Dad to conduct, and he agreed, but he did not belong to the Toronto Musicians Association, or TMA – a member and affiliate of the American Federation of Musicians, or AFM, a powerful body. The head of the Toronto branch called Dad and told him that he would have to join TMA or there would be no concert. Dad had never found it necessary or helpful to be a member of the union. The fee to join was considerable; Dad was conducting pro bono for a one-time thing and felt that he had no need for union protection under normal circumstances. The telephone calls became acrimonious. Mother put her hands over my ears and shooed me out to play. Eventually Dad realized that in order for the musicians to work he would have to join. He then had to receive pay, and he took the lowest rate. Harold Sumberg was the first concertmaster for the Proms. The first year was not exactly a moneymaker.

When the AFM musicians' journal arrived by mail, Dad disdained to touch it, but I scanned it for familiar names. I could then regale my chums at school about which of the popular jazz conductors – the Dorseys, Louis Armstrong, Rudy Vallee – were in trouble for underpaying their players or had otherwise run afoul of union rules. Since band leaders were the equivalent of today's rock stars, this was juicy inside stuff to my teenaged audience.

The next summer there were to be more Promenade Concerts. This time Mother suggested having them in a place where the audience could go outside in the intermission for fresh air – air conditioning had yet to arrive. It so happened that Uncle Leo Stokowski was in town and was coming for lunch. He came up with a brilliant suggestion: the hockey arena at the university. Dad was sceptical: "Let's go down there and try it out." He telephoned to arrange for someone to unlock the facility. Uncle Leo rummaged through Mother's tool basket and chose two of her hammers, and off the two men went to test the reverberations in the arena. Mother shook her head. They were behaving like a couple of young students. She went on preparing lunch. They soon returned, both elated. "A perfect symphony hall," Uncle Leo pronounced in that wonderful accent of his. "Reverbs are perfect," added Dad. They must have had a great old time hammering away at either end of the arena to test the sound patterns of the place.

Dad did not want to conduct for the second summer. He was busy working on his Symphony No. 1 but did have a pupil whom he considered ready for the job, Reginald Stewart. Reggie continued on for years, growing in experience, and left finally to conduct the Baltimore Symphony. He did conduct the première of Symphony No. 1 on a hot evening in August 1936. At the concert, the young woman in the seat directly in front of Bunny asked her date how one goes about writing a symphony. According to the young man, it was really very simple – just putting down notes on a page and letting the musicians play them. My brother and I started to laugh. For months we had all lived, eaten, slept Symphony No. 1. I earned five cents a page scoring bar lines on music manuscript paper about two feet high. I learned to use a mapping pen and a T square. It is not easy work. Manuscript paper is very expensive, and one tiny blot ruins the whole page. An inadvertent dot can have repercussions!

Mother and Dad sat in the front row in the red seats for 75 cents, Bunny and I in the greys for 50 cents, and the greens were 25 cents. This made a great date for cash-pressed young people, 50 cents for a pair of tickets and an ice-cream Eskimo Pie for 10 cents in the intermission. With streetcar tickets four for a dollar, one could have an evening out for well under two dollars. The Proms became so popular that the transit authority put extra streetcars on Bloor on Prom nights to handle the crowds – a first for 'classical' music in Toronto.

I now had the front bedroom in the attic, and Dad's baby grand, where he composed, was right below me. I went to sleep listening to the themes and frequently woke up early in the morning to the same ones. Dad played a theme again and again, subtle changes in emphasis, all the while hearing different voices of the orchestra playing it, chiming in, or supporting it. There were breakfasts when he handed over a few pages of full orchestral score to Mother. They both read full scores the way the rest of us read newspapers. One should read a full score up and down and left and right at more or less the same time and hear the melodies simultaneously in one's head! Sometimes Mother's comments were hardly complimentary. She was a true critic, harsh, if necessary, but good.

"Healey, you can't have the trombones and French horns together like this." "Shouldn't there be space here for these winds to get a breath?" Suggestions came, but never more than one at a time. Mother was a diplomat as well as a critic. Sometimes Dad would storm out upstairs and Mother would mutter, "That man, why can't he listen to me? I know I'm right." Sometimes Mother stormed out to the kitchen or the garden, muttering under her breath. Later in the day he would show up with more work. "Oh, Healey, this is splendid. Yes. I do like what you have done with this part." No other words; she knew that he had heard her after all, and they were both happy.

I was going through a muted-string phase. "Please, Daddy, put something in for muted strings, maybe in the slow movement?" He humphed a bit. There are no passages for muted strings in Symphony No. 1, but in sorting out his manuscripts after his death Giles and I did find a page or so, suitable key signature. So perhaps he did write a little something for his bar-line scribe and then, thoroughgoing professional, tossed it into a drawer and forgot all about it.

Usually after breakfast, when the brothers, and then I too, had all cleared out for school, Dad went upstairs to bathe and dress. He must have liked to work out musical themes and plan works in general in a hot, misty atmosphere in the tub. When he was working on something that he wanted to talk about, he would summon Mother, and she would drop whatever she was doing – working on her books or just plain household tasks. Often it was with reluctance that I saw her trail upstairs to the steamy bathroom and perch on the throne, with Dad holding court in watery state. This was their version of what other couples call 'pillow talk.' It often lasted an hour or more, depending on Dad's lecture and teaching schedule. As the water cooled, he replaced it with hot, and when Mother finally emerged from her steam immersion she would be wiping her brow.

Most of Mother's friends were creative types, musicians, writers, and artists, and many of them visited 139 at teatime. Reaching home after school, I would sometimes find Mother and Katharine Hale, the writer, having tea together. Their conversation usually centred on what they were reading and who was writing for *Saturday Night*. Lady Willison, writer, editor, and widow of Sir John, the influential journalist and historian, was another guest, and talk focused on current events. Another time Mother's guest might be Mary White, with her accounts of the latest stories and general goings-on in the newsroom at the *Mail and Empire*. White's pseudonym was 'Bride Broder,' and she covered, among other items, the farmers' offerings at the St Lawrence Market on Saturday mornings. This meant that she was on her job about 4.30 a.m. on Saturday, preparing her copy on the freshest vegetables and fruits and the price of butter and eggs. She filed her piece well before 6 a.m. so that it would reach the first edition in time for Toronto's breakfast tables. It was a daunting job, but she loved it. She was more than capable of covering a war or a juicy court case but had to handle the price of lettuce.

Another of Mother's friends, Kate Miles, had served as a nurse in France in the Great War and received the Mons Star Medal for bravery under fire. She ran the Little Trinity Housekeeping Centre in the rectory of Little Trinity Church on King Street East in 'The Ward.' The minister lived elsewhere, and during the Depression the congregation converted the rectory into a drop-in centre. The facility sought to help mothers and to keep children off the street after school. The boys were apt to break into factory yards to steal coal for their desperate families. The converted rectory needed volunteers, so Mother, a member of the board of the Housekeeping Centre, said that I could take charge once a week of a group of boys, aged from about 10 to 16.

I was only 14. What on earth could I do to engage their interest? I thought about my charges and what their lives must be like, as if I knew what it is to go to sleep cold and hungry and wake even colder and hungrier. I wondered if they would enjoy tales of heroic deeds and overcoming obstacles, bravery under fire, general excitement. Up in the attic I knew that we had a stash of the brothers' leftover *Boys Own Annual*s and *Chums*. I dug them out and started reading the sort of stories that I thought might distract the boys from their own misery.

I had promised to take on the job, but only if I had a supply of paints, brushes, crayons, plenty of paper. Mother called on her old friend Col. R.Y. Eaton and explained the situation, and he came through handsomely. My requirements arrived by Eaton's delivery van. My teaching arrangement was simple enough. I told the young fellows a story that I had read in those annuals, plenty of scope in them, and then I asked them to tell me a story, anything they wanted – an illustration of what I had told them about or just anything that they fancied. It worked like a charm, and I don't think that the oldest ones realized that 'teacher' was younger than they were. I kept them at it until 5.30 or 6 p.m., when we served them cocoa and peanut-butter sandwiches, gifts from a dairy and a bakery, respectively. For some of them it may have been the biggest meal of the day.

Probably in 1934 Mother cajoled the beautiful, elegant, aptly named Angela, wife of Lieutenant-Governor Dr Herbert Bruce, to visit Cabbagetown to see what life was like there. She arrived in a shiny, chauffeur-driven automobile, wearing a fur coat and looking regal. This apparition impressed my pupils, who lined up to meet her. She shook hands with them all and gave each a good-sized chocolate bar, which *really* impressed them. One of my youngest tried to slip back into line for another chocolate bar; he was a funny little monkey, and the vicereine recognized him at once.

Teaching my class art was a learning experience for me and I hope for them. The same little monkey refused one winter afternoon to take off his rubber boots, just 'wellies.' When finally Miss Miles insisted, it turned out that he had no socks, just unlined rubber boots. One day I asked her about how three boys, all with different surnames and about the same age, could look so much alike. Were they cousins, perhaps? She smiled and said, "Think about it." Some of the neighbourhood men would find the odd job, seasonal work, that kept them out of town for a couple of weeks at a time, and some were doing time in jail or in prison. "Oh," I said. "I see what you mean."

The young fellows ostracized one lad who was having a difficult time. His father was doing time in jail for breaking a shop window and stealing a loaf of bread from the window – a 'break' with no 'entry.' His wife had just given birth, their living quarters were cold, and they had no food and no money. He had been a hardrock miner in northern Ontario. Now, out of work when the mine closed, he moved his family to the big city, thinking that there must be something that a strong back could receive pay to work at. Because he was not a resident of Toronto, he had been ineligible for relief. Miss Miles did what she could with my group to help his young son.

Mother thought that a piano would improve the Little Trinity Centre, and so Col. Eaton heard from her again. An upright arrived, and someone tuned it. Mother used to go a couple of mornings a week to play for the women as they cut and hemmed bolts of muslin, courtesy of Col. Eaton, into sheets. Mother told me that some of the women cried. It was the first time that they were going to have sheets on their beds since they married. Col. Eaton would sometimes greet Mother at parties with a smile and a query: "What do you have in mind for your centre this week?"

Overhearing some of the women at the centre chatting about their husbands' political views, rather anarchistic, Mother decided to hold an open-air tea party in our garden before the upcoming provincial election. Our riding stretched north from the lakeshore east of Yonge Street to Moore Park, where we lived, and it included Little Trinity. Mother invited the entire sheet-trimming set and approached Uncle Roly Michener, a Tory, who accepted her invitation to speak about the Conservative platform. His speech was good and went down well. There were intelligent questions, and the guests enjoyed talking with a real, live politician. The next morning an armful of red roses with stems about three feet long arrived for Mother from Uncle Roly. He later won election to both the provincial legislature and the House of Commons in Ottawa, where he became Speaker; he eventually served as Canada's high commissioner to India, and governor general. Coffee parties in people's homes became a popular election strategy in bad times and good.

Many of the young men from my class at the centre joined up in 1939 as soon as war began, gaining regular pay for the first time in their lives. A number of them never made it back home, I am sure.

One bitter January morning in the mid-1930s our postman, Mr Southorn, instead of dropping our mail through the slot on the front door, knocked. There was a registered letter that someone had to sign for, not all that unusual an occurrence. We were having breakfast, and it was so cold outside that Mother invited him in for a cup of tea. Mr Southorn replied that he didn't drink tea but would appreciate a cup of coffee. This was after our last live-in had moved on and before Mrs Hosie showed up to begin working that day. So Mother padded out to the kitchen to make him coffee, and he dumped his mail bag in the living-room, drew up a chair beside Dad, and made conversation, mainly about the weather, a vital concern to him of course. He addressed my father as 'Professor,' a title that Dad hated, which he had probably picked up from letters, but when someone places your sorted mail beside your plate it is impossible to be unfriendly.

Mr Southorn was invariably cheery. He did enjoy Mother's coffee and thereafter sat down with us every single breakfast until he retired long after the end of the Second World War. First the knock, the entrance – he just let himself in – the whump of the mailbag in the living-room, and his march around the table delivering our mail individually, officially launching our day. He sat himself down always at the same place, his place, and enjoyed his coffee. He arrived six days a week, including Saturday.

He took great pride in the foreign stamps on the professor's mail. One time he handed Dad an envelope for 'Dr. Healey Willan, Composer, Canada.' One Saturday morning – I was a teenager and had been to a party the night before – he handed me my mail and upbraided me for coming down to breakfast in my night clothes. Sometimes we picked up gossip, useful or not – who was moving, whose dog was in trouble with the dogcatcher – real village news. Dad grew to forgive him the 'professor' bit, and they chatted in genuine affection for each other.

If we were out back, Mr Southorn just walked through the house without a disturbing knock, and his coffee was always ready and waiting for him. In the summertime we always ate outdoors on the back porch, which the neighbours found odd. We wrapped blankets around our knees to encourage the end of spring and later to confront autumn. It was Mr Southorn who noticed at some stage that our wooden porch was in serious need of some reconstruction. The posts had given in to old age and were about to crumble into rot at their bases. The war was heating up; lumber, nails, and paint were all hard to come by, and labour for such non-essential work was even harder. Mr Southorn said that he and his brother would take care of it. The two spent a week of their summer vacations making our old porch shipshape. Mother never asked where they obtained the supplies, and the prices were what one would reasonably expect to pay, not at black-market levels. More Torontonians began eating outdoors after the war, when returning troops introduced the custom from France and Italy.

The only time that I remember anything really upsetting Mr Southorn was on Dad's 80th birthday, October 12, 1960. He had no mail for the professor on his birthday, which concerned him. Coffee was still on of course, and we had all settled nicely when postal officials knocked on the door. They dumped two sacks of birthday cards alongside Mr Southorn's bag, which in fact made our friend, after he calmed down, still prouder to be the professor's 'postie.' Dad answered every single card; he felt that anybody who had taken the trouble to find a card, compose a message, stamp it, and mail it should receive the courtesy of a thank you.

During the Depression, our front porch sprouted inconspicuous chalk marks. Wash them off, neighbours advised Mother. Those marks told every passing hobo that our house was good for a handout of food. Mother refused. While we have enough at home to share, we will share, was her response.

Sometimes a man would mumble his thanks, and once in a while, on a nasty cold or wet day, someone would come into the kitchen to eat and to warm himself. We heard about what had been happening – mines that had shut down and miners knowing no other trade, people from closed-up factories, and others who knew no trade, fresh out of school or college, hitchhiking to the city hoping for any kind of work. Occasionally a veteran would tell us about the unimaginable horrors of the trenches in France.

City hall was not being mean: it simply had very little money. Men might tell us about various trades and occupations that they had been in before these hard times, but there was simply no hiring and there was no relief for those passing through town. We knew of a few people on relief who lived in big houses; they had to pay realty taxes or lose their only asset after the stock-market crash. They had to eat too, and who would buy their homes if they put them on the market?

Dad practised on the organ in the very cold loft at St Mary Magdalene's, with reduced heating to save money. Chest colds were part of his winters, and a cassock helped to keep his legs warm. He would arrive home to a cup of 'ram's wool' – a traditional Yorkshire concoction of warm milk and a dollop of scotch – to take away some of the chill. It didn't help the family finances when Dad, more than once I gather, paid the rent for a bass or a tenor who had suddenly lost his job – he simply needed the voice in the choir. "Make do, make over, make mend" was a phrase that we all knew. Mother's favourite: "If there's a remedy, try and find it. If there's none, never mind it." It was a preparation in a way for the even-tougher times of the coming war. There would be more money but more anxiety, and the workload was heavy.

At one Evensong during the depths of the Depression, the metropolitan of the Greek Orthodox church preached at St Mary's. His golden robes and cope were eye-catching, a feast for the eyes. When I travel abroad and encounter magnificent vestments, tapestries, or works of art in communities where people are anything but rich, I sometimes think of the visiting prelate and the pleasure that his magnificence gave us in a time of scarcity.

CHAPTER TEN

Grenville Street and the Arts and Letters (1935–1939)

At the Toronto Conservatory of Music, Dad had been since 1913 an instructor and since 1920 vice-principal. He was also trying to provide a decent standard of living for his family on what had been a laughably meagre salary anyway. The governors of the music school, all businessmen of considerable means, did not relate salaries in the institution with the cost of living. Perhaps they considered teaching music a kind of fringe benefit for the wealthy and not a serious profession. In 1936 my father left the conservatory after almost a quarter-century of service there.

Sir Ernest MacMillan had the Toronto Symphony Orchestra, the Toronto Mendelssohn Choir, and examining jobs in western Canada for Britain's Royal College of Music. Dad had St Mary's, composing, and examining for the conservatory. British, German, and American publishers were offering him contracts to compose specific works, and he received royalties on sales of sheet music, performing rights, and mechanical rights on the new thing – records.

By June of every year the wicker basket in his study was overflowing with contracts, very often for Christmas compositions. At 139 Inglewood Drive, Christmas started in June on the grand piano in Dad's study. In 1935, the brothers having left the nest, I moved into the bedroom above my father's piano; my hearing him at work – until I married and moved out in 1943 – would prove invaluable decades later. And Christmas music was rampant, late at night and first thing in the morning as Dad prepared for Convocation in early June, examining in western Canada, and then summer schools in the United States. Each Christmas at Midnight Mass, as I mentioned above, Mother used to tell me to listen really well to this new work – "quite the best your father has written." She said the same thing every year.

Dad left the conservatory under very trying circumstances in 1936, and the next year he became professor of music in the Faculty of Music in the University of Toronto. His salary started off low; as he grew older, the bean counters must have figured that he probably would not leave, so they had no incentive to increase it.

How little they knew. In the late 1930s, Dr M.M. Moore of the University of Michigan at Ann Arbor approached Dad. He visited the house several times. Mother and I both liked him very much. In Ann Arbor, Dad would have had many more opportunities to hear his works in performances, especially as he was turning to larger compositions – symphonies and operas, something vital to a composer. Mother and I were on the point of packing for Michigan when Dad suddenly changed his mind. Leaving Canada, with its ties to his homeland and another war looming, which would involve his children, was just not on. The reversal saddened Mother and me somewhat.

Dad had also taught repeatedly at the summer school of the University of California at Los Angeles, and for a while that city seemed a real possibility for us. Dad spent entire summers there, which allowed me to fine-tune my reading skills. After earlier using Mother's *Jesu, Joy of Man's Desiring* and then going on to Dad's score of *Parsifal* and success, I now had his library all to myself.

Shortly before the Second World War, Dad received expressions of interest from yet another music faculty, at McGill University. Mother told me that we might be packing up for Montreal, which prospect pleased her. Her sister, Aunt Edie, and Uncle Gordon Church lived there, and an old friend of hers, Dorothy King, taught music at McGill. Again we were almost on our way when the deal fell through. Gossip being what it is, word soon reached Mother that the visiting dean of music, in Toronto apparently to entice Dad to McGill, learned that Dad was, if not an alcoholic, the next thing to it. This story outraged Mother.

Many years later, after Mother's death, I asked Dad about the sudden abandonment of McGill, and he more or less reiterated the story that Mother heard. Dad permitted himself a slight but sad smile as he told me that the husband of the female misinformer, now reaching the end of his life, had become "overmuch dependent on a drink." So, as Dad would say, there we are. The huge cache of unopened bottles that my brothers and I found in the cellar after Dad's death – the 80th-birthday gift of 80 bottles, most of them wine – gave the lie to that allegation.

In 1936–37, the year between the conservatory and the faculty, Dad rented a studio on Grenville Street, near the university. Archie MacDonald and Franz Johnston had studios in the same building, and Dad felt right at home working alongside those two merrymakers. The day Dad moved in, Archie, by way of welcome, made an impassioned speech from his second-storey balcony to non-existent crowds, presumably cheering in the street below, a lively figure in his usual kilt. His mother was a sculptor, and he created stained-glass windows, normally for churches. He once claimed a remote island somewhere between Greenland and Baffin Island for Canada in a suitably dramatic ceremony by hammering a ten-cent piece into a rock, royal-face-side up. Presumably the island, probably more of a shoal, is part of Canada anyway, but he loved to recount his story, with a wicked gleam in his eye, looking every bit a medieval Scottish warrior in that kilt.

Franz Johnston was originally 'Frank' but became a fervent believer in numerology after he had dropped off the 'k' and replaced it with a 'z.' It all happened at the same time that his wife needed an urgent operation, which was to cost $200. There was no medicare or OHIP back then, and Mr Johnston told me that he had no idea where to obtain so much money. A friend had been reading about numerology and suggested that they add up the letters of his name. Not too propitious, said the friend, but wait. If we take out the 'k' and substitute 'z,' it gets much luckier. The artist shrugged and gestured with both hands as he was talking.

"What's to lose, I said, so I changed the very next canvas to sign it 'Franz Johnston.'" A day later, a possible customer had arrived at Grenville Street in a sleek, shiny black Cadillac. She was the wife of a mining magnate, according to Franz, and she was looking for something special as a birthday surprise for her husband. She thought that a picture of the northern forests that he loved so much would do it. She spent a long time looking over every winter landscape that Johnston had, finally pointing at a snowy landscape with bright blue sky, sunshine, purple shadows on the snow, and dark-green pine trees. She said that it was just the thing that she had in mind, except … The painter's heart beat quickened and then fell.

"If it only had a dog team racing across the front," she said, "it would be perfect." Johnston recovered in a flash and told her that he did have something in the back, very similar in style and subject, same arrangement of trees, blue sky, white snow, lots of purple shadows, and yes, now that he came to think of it, it did have a dog team. So if she would like to return the next day, he could have it out for her to view.

The wily painter started up the minute the door closed. He worked hard and fast. As they had arranged, the woman was back the next day, loved it, and paid for it in cash – $200, of course. Johnston recalled that he had commented to Dad and Archie MacDonald, "I hope she doesn't try to pet those damned dogs. They won't be dry for a couple of days more." He wound up the story by saying that he didn't hear anything about smudged dogs, so he assumed that the birthday gift went down a treat. Mrs Johnston's surgery was a success. From then on, he told me, he was to be Franz.

At the front of a gracious old residence on Grenville Street, Mr Malloney rented out rooms as studios, and in the rear he had turned the former ballroom into the Malloney Galleries, an exhibit hall for his tenants and other artists in the neighbourhood. One Saturday morning when Franz Johnston's paintings filled the entire hall, the artist took me around his show, talking about each canvas, where he had done it, how he felt about it, whether it satisfied him completely or just partially, and what had attracted him to a particular lookout. After these thorough explanations, he asked me which one I liked best. That was easy. In all those outstanding pieces, my favourite was a snow scene at dusk, with snowflakes falling gently and the only warmth visible a couple of faint, blurry, pink-tinged windows off in the distance. I asked him how he obtained that effect of a snowfall without daubing bits of white paint all over, and he replied, "I don't know. I honestly do not know. I would love to get that effect again, but I don't know how I did it." Then he smiled. "It's my favourite too."

I often dropped into the studios on Grenville Street, not quite on my way home from school, but a warm, cheery place to be. Dad sometimes handed me little things that musicians, students, droppers-in would give him after their travels. Once he gave me a *matrioshka* doll, the *baba* of the group and quite old, that Boris Berlin had given him on his return from the Soviet Union. "I thought only card-carrying Communists could get into the USSR," I said. Dad merely shrugged, with that hands-spread gesture of who knows? It was a mystery. Boris Berlin was the teacher at the conservatory who had cribbed Mother's stuff from her *Manual of Ear-Training and Sight-Singing*. I had only to admire some little ornament in his studio, and Dad would say, "Take it." So I took the antique doll home.

Archie MacDonald married Billy Button, Henry Button's daughter. Mr Button was in charge of a bookshop that had some connection with Oxford University Press. It was on Bloor Street opposite the old Political Science building, which is now the Royal Conservatory of Music. The bookshop was a replica of a structure in Oxford and had an inviting fake-Tudor front and carved oak inside – a wonderful place to spend a couple of hours.

Mr Button was a member of the Arts and Letters, which presented many entertainments. A benefit for Augustus Bridle, music critic at the *Toronto Daily Star*, was an all-male version of *The Beggar's Opera (or an Executive Year)*. Perhaps Gus Bridle was the club treasurer that year. It must have been a hilarious spoof, with Dad as MacHeath and the portly Henry Button as Polly. Arthur Lismer played Hangman; J.E.H. Macdonald, the son of MacHeath; Lawrence Harris, Pot Boy; and Ernest MacMillan, Tim Whistle! Hector Charlesworth was Peacham.

Every president of the club had a 'coat of arms,' rather more like an apron with a design by J.E.H. Macdonald, and wore it as a sort of symbolic bib over the chest. Mr Button's of course had a four-holed button on a portion of a chessboard. Dr MacCallum's was a rather stylized tree bent to the wind. He was the hospitable owner of the cottage on Georgian Bay where various members of the Group of Seven stayed and painted. Tom Thomson painted his iconic *West Wind* there. I never knew what was on Dad's apron, and I have never seen it on display at the club with the others. It never came home. This was very definitely an all-male club.

Wives and interested parties were welcome at an annual outpouring of high spirits – Toronto's signal that spring had finally arrived. Napier Moore, the editor of *Maclean's Magazine*, devised it as *April Foolies*. Later it was just *The Spring Revue*. It lasted from the 1920s to sometime during the Second World War, when lightheartedness was an especially cherished and essential commodity. Tickets were hard to come by – everybody wanted to see what the town's most brilliant wits had cooked up.

I would hear bits of what Dad was writing before opening night and Mother's appreciative comments afterwards. It was just as much a springtime ritual as shucking snowboots or taking down the storm windows. Since women were welcome in the audience and Nella Jefferis took part at least once in the later years, the skits reflected their presence, and the resulting omission of anything 'off-colour' did not decrease the hilarity.

In one of the club's pre-Christmas entertainments, Scott Malcolm, one half of the acclaimed Malcolm and Godden two-piano team, was going to play Mendelssohn writing *Hark the Herald Angels Sing,* and there was a tiny part for me. Reg Godden and Scott Malcolm were often in and out of 139, and then we wouldn't see them for weeks. "Oh, the boys are on tour," I would hear. South America this time, or perhaps Japan or Town Hall in New York.

For the club's show, an angel was to inspire the composer, as Mendelssohn alleged happened. Dad told me at breakfast one day that I had the role, which was a surprise to me, and to report to the club for rehearsal the next day after school. He had told Scott Malcolm that I would do. I suspect that long blonde hair had something to do with the casting. It was all very simple. All I had to do was appear with arms and wings outspread in some kind of long white getup and just watch Malcolm play, preferably with an approving smile.

I had heard of stage fright of course. Dad would become grumpy, Mother would take it all with immense calm, outwardly at any rate, and I would go into a deep freeze. Scott Malcolm shook from head to toe. I have never seen anything like it. He seemed to be coming apart, literally. But the millisecond his foot was out of the wings he was in complete control and thoroughly professional, a transformation indeed.

Sometime in the 1930s, Dad brought home an oil sketch from the club. One of the members had gone sketching out west all summer and had hung his pieces, price $25 each, in hopes of a few sales. I am fairly sure that the artist was one of the Group of Seven, but he did not sign it. Dad both liked the sketch and wanted to help the painter. Mother didn't think much of it – she was not particularly fond of the Group, although she liked Arthur Lismer, both the man and his work. Hector Charlesworth called the Group the 'Hot Mush School,' and she tended to agree.

The sketch went upstairs to the trunk room. By the time I found it years later, we had all forgotten who the artist was, if we had ever known. A.Y. Jackson said that it wasn't his, although it could have been, except he wasn't out west that summer. A.J. Casson tried to place it and gave up. So there it is, artist unknown. "If you like it, take it," Dad said, so I did.

Dr Jackson made a quick sketch of Dad for me one day on the back of a catalogue of a show of Maurice Cullen's work in the Art Gallery of Hamilton, but he forgot an ear. When we met at the McMichael Gallery in Kleinburg for tea, probably sometime after Dad's death in 1968, I took the one-eared sketch with me, and he said, "Oh, yes, your father had big ears, didn't he?" and he drew the other one at a stroke. We walked together through his works at the McMichael. He was particularly keen on talking about the items that he had done as a war artist in the Great War, and in no time at all we had a respectful entourage following behind, close enough to hear him, but not intrusive. I heard later that near the end of his life he did enjoy walking through the gallery talking about his paintings and reliving the circumstances of their creation.

It seemed to me that Dad heard something rhythmical in everything from a dripping tap to an impatient driver honking a horn. When we headed out to the streetcar together, he had me walk at a different pace to his, and we both had to keep abreast. It was one way to learn about counterpoint. Then he would say, "Let's make this into a tune, you have this one and I'll do the first part." It keeps you on your toes, literally and figuratively. It was all as natural to him as breathing in and out, which I am sure he put to music from time to time. He could make the same progression of notes jollity itself or infinitely sad.

Once he spoke to the students at Moulton College for girls, on Bloor Street East, where Manufacturers Life now faces St Paul's Anglican. According to one of my friends who was studying there, Dad charmed them right from the start by asking them to name their favourite tune from the hit parade. *Mairzy Doats* won by a landslide. Dad played the melody through, then changed beats, changed key signature, turned it into a fugue, played the melody back to front, then a march, on and on. He had fun playing with the song, turning it inside out and upside down, and his young audience sang along with him and apparently had a great morning.

Dad told me of going to an orchestral rehearsal in England as a young student. The Russian conductor Artur Nikisch, his hero, was conducting the London Symphony in Tchaikowsky's Pathétique symphony. Just before the end of the second movement, he stopped the orchestra and commented in his thick accent, "No, no, this is not a little break-up, this is the heartbreak of the whole world." Dad choked up when he told me of it. After so many years, his memory of what he had learned, the effects of Nikisch's words, was still fresh and keen. The orchestra played the same notes on the repeat, but infinitely more affecting. It made me want to listen to all music with more attention. Was the conductor really bringing to life the intention, the meaning, of what the composer wanted the listener to experience – yearning, abject sorrow, over-the-top exuberance, whatever – by the little black notes on five horizontal lines?

At breakfast one morning in the mid-1930s, Dad sat down a little late and hadn't done the crossword puzzle. Sleeping in was not something that he usually did. He admitted that he had arrived home a bit before 3.30 a.m., but not much. By now we were all curious, especially Mother. Dad explained that a few of his students had been the previous evening at the Brass Rail, a favourite watering hole for Toronto Mendelssohn Choir members and students from the music faculty after a rehearsal in Massey Hall. They had heard a well-known blues combo, which really impressed them – so much so that they begged my father to join them the next night. He told us that he demurred – had a lot of work to catch up on and so on – but they were persuasive.

After a couple of sets the musicians' spontaneity had entranced him. He particularly liked the way each player would take up a solo, and then, perfectly smoothly, another would take over and just extemporize on the theme. After closing time, Dad, the group, and his students did some serious jamming for hours. No wonder he was exhausted.

At the time there was a contract in Dad's wicker basket from Carl Fischer, the New York publisher, for a Christmas motet. Even as he spoke about his jamming, I think, his setting of *Hodie, Christus natus est* (c. 1935) was already coming to life in his head, for he finished it very soon. It has a beautiful blues harmonization and a syncopation that do not occur in his other Christmas motets. As I mention above, there is a little black dot in the score, which conductors easily overlook.

Sometimes at breakfast on a Wednesday, Dad regaled Mother and me with recounting the discussion at Tuesday lunch, the day before, a most informal gathering at the Mary John Tea Room on College Street, where the nurses' residence is now. Insulin discoverers Dr Frederick ('Freddy') Banting and Dr Charles ('Charley') Best, Dr Gordon Murray, and a few non-physicians from the university all showed up from time to time, as their schedules permitted. They talked of ideas, politics, whatever subject anyone brought up. There was one proviso: when the discussion centred on your own discipline, you had to listen, not participate.

Most of the Tuesday people were doctors. Dad and Freddy seemed to be two of the most compatible. The meeting place was convenient for Dad, just down the street from the conservatory, as it was for staff people from the Toronto General. When Sir Frederick Banting flew off to Britain during the war and died after his plane crashed, many questions surfaced. Many people thought that he was working on something top-secret for the war effort, and the crash was a mystery.

One morning Dad was gathering receipts and all the paper work to take down to George McCann, his lawyer, for income-tax preparation. He couldn't find a statement from the CBC for a commissioned work that it had broadcast some months earlier. He checked his bankbook – no record of deposit. He checked all the papers that he had collected. The cheque should have had a date about eight months earlier, according to the terms of the contract.

With that look of his that presaged battle ahead, Dad picked up the phone, called the CBC, and asked to speak to the treasurer. After a pleasant greeting, Dad said that he was truly sorry to understand that the CBC was in bankruptcy. That caught the official's attention. There was anguished muttering and the declaration that this rumour was definitely untrue. "Oh," said Dad, "I assumed you must be facing serious financial problems, as you have not paid me for work I have completed and which you used some months ago." It sounded like more muffled blustering on the other end of the line, but on friendly terms Dad wished the treasurer a good day and put down the receiver. The cheque arrived the next day, and Dad made a new appointment to see McCann.

"Just complaining doesn't get you far. You have to grab their attention, and always go to the top," was his fatherly advice to me. Just as he had previously advised me when crossing an international border and answering questions, give the briefest answer possible and make sure that your answer does not give rise to a further query. This piece of advice surfaced when Dad returned home from some U.S. event via train from New York. A customs officer asked him what he did. I write music, was the answer. The officer, after being a bit officious, then told Dad that he wrote music too and asked for some pointers.

At one of our many conversations at the dining-room table at home, Dad recounted a rehearsal that he had just attended in the theatre of the Royal Ontario Museum. It was for a first performance of something that Igor Stravinsky had just written, and the composer was conducting. At one point a French-horn player had spoken and pointed out to him that the notes he had written for his instrument were impossible to play, probably from a breathing standpoint. Stravinsky, in exasperation – the rehearsal was not going well – shouted something like, "Play whatever you want. It doesn't matter. Nobody will hear you anyway."

Dad was still in shock. Melody for him was the very basis of all music, and to dismiss a player's justified comment like that – he just shook his head. Mother was in complete agreement. She had taken me to Massey Hall to hear Paderewski and Kreisler, warning me that I might hear a wrong note – they were both well past their best years – but to listen to their techniques and their interpretations, each in his way a colossal master of his instrument. And here was what the world was coming to – a composer who didn't care what notes an instrumentalist played, soloist or not, or even whether the notes on the score were playable. It was incomprehensible to her.

One of Dad's publishers, Walter Hinrichsen, head of the New York office of C.F. Peters, visited Toronto at least once a year to discuss new works with Dad. He and his wife always stayed at the Royal York Hotel and always asked my parents to lunch with them there. In the charming European tradition, they always sent flowers to Mother the following day as a thank you for her presence. One time, they sent a rubber plant instead. It went on our second-floor landing, with a south and east exposure, and it thrived. Year by year, 'Walter' headed straight for the ceiling. Some people suggested that we cut a hole in the ceiling for the tree to grow up into the third floor – my bedroom, as it happened. I was not keen on that. Mother had its top trimmed, but nothing deterred Walter. It kept right on pretending to be in a jungle for well over twenty years. It gave up and slowly withered only after Mother died. She loved Walter, and they do say that plants form an attachment to the people who give them water and care.

In London, Mother had known as a neighbour Mark Hambourg, a pianist with an international reputation. In Canada, his brothers Boris and Jan established the Toronto Music Lover's Club, offering concerts by the de Kresz–Hambourg Trio, the Pirani Trio, and the Pro Musica. Chamber music was popular, and many people attended the recitals. Michael Hambourg, their father, had established the Hambourg Conservatoire in London and later transferred it to Toronto as the Hambourg Conservatory. The family brought with it the lively sort of European insouciance that staid Toronto had lacked.

The Depression hit the Hambourgs' establishment harder than the Toronto Conservatory. Boris and his wife, Maria, whom my parents knew, found it very difficult to make ends meet, as I was to see up close. At some time in the mid-1930s, Mother and Dad received an invitation to a cocktail party at the home of Mrs Wallace Barrett, a well-known patron of the arts. It was probably in honour of some musical lion. Dad refused to go. He hated that sort of event and probably knew the 'lion' anyway.

Mother looked me up and down. I was just a teenager, but she must have thought that I would pass, as she had no intention of going alone. So it was my unofficial debut to Toronto high society. I had never been in such a large and ornate home, with one maid to open the door for us, and another to take our coats. Then we crossed a grand reception area. Mrs Barrett received her guests in a proper lineup at the bottom of the steps into her sunken living-room. I followed Mother, caught my heel on a small oriental carpet at the foot of the steps, and skidded past Mrs Barrett and her guest at a rate considerably faster than walking pace.

This displeased Mother, and I soon found myself in a conservatory more or less out of sight. Boris Hambourg came leering over. Maria's eyes were black anyway and could be intense at the best of times, and now she was glaring at me. Boris had no idea that Healey's little girl had grown into an interesting specimen. He confronted me, and I backed up. In fact we did a sort of fandango, with Boris advancing and me retreating around a coffee table at least three times. The only pause occurred when a maid came around with a tray of sandwiches. Boris stuffed a handful into his jacket pocket. Maria filled her handbag, a well-known habit of hers, I learned.

When I complained to Mother later at home about Boris and his creepy advances, her only comment was that I should know how to take care of myself. But that was a tall order for a teenager in the face of a lecherous old boy, a colleague of one's father, along with a jealous wife about to explode. Mother told me as well that the sandwiches in the handbag probably constituted their dinner that evening.

In the long run, perhaps 139 Inglewood turned out to be a good buy for my family. There were many empty lots nearby ripe for development, which did indeed happen. Ditches disappeared one by one as the city paved streets in the early 1920s. Our Lady of Perpetual Help School on Clifton Road overlooked the ravine (Avoca Vale). In the 1930s, it extended its playing fields over part of the ravine with an authorized garbage dump. Rats discovered an opportunity to share in the suburban way of life. They found this an ideal housing site, with humans delivering new edibles to the premises five days a week, a park to play in, and a stream nearby of fresh running water.

The rats received the surprise of their lives in the late 1930s, when suddenly free home delivery ceased, construction dirt arrived by the truckload on top of them, and steamrollers crushed their warrens while flattening out the earth for the school's new baseball field. The rodents made a pilgrimage into the surrounding streets, and every house soon seethed with rat traps. Neighbourhood chitchat compared tunnels between floors and walls and the noises of platoons of little feet running up and down inside the walls. Occasionally a rat homicide occurred. The little creatures did fight for property rights down in the cellars and up under the roofs. Sometimes old age accounted for a corpse. Either way, the unfortunate homeowner then had to take up floorboards and break down walls to remove the remains.

Young neighbours loved to watch rats fight in the gutters, but I never heard of the beasties' biting anyone. The rats' hegira lasted until war erupted between them in front of 139. Mother telephoned the Humane Society, which directed her to the city's department of health. The conflict involved six or seven rats. The children of

Red Horner, the hockey player, who lived next door, were down on their knees rooting for their team. The employee at the health department asked, "Madam, don't you know there is a real war going on?" Mother replied that she was well aware of what was happening in Europe, but rats fighting in a residential street in broad daylight surely merited some attention. Eventually someone called the Horner kids in to lunch. There was some kind of ceasefire, and the Humane Society arrived to pick up the casualties.

Trixie, a smooth-haired fox terrier, was our family pet at the time. At mealtimes she set herself under the dining-room table. A raw apple would keep her busy and contented. Suddenly the chewing sound underneath the table might cease, and Trixie tiptoed through to the cellar door, which we kept open for her convenience. A few minutes later she would come pattering upstairs to the side door. Then one of us would open the door for her, and she would dig a hole to bury the deceased.

I tiptoed downstairs after her one evening to study her method. She stood like a statue near a hole (new holes appeared frequently right at the outside basement walls). When an unobservant rat wandered past her, she grabbed it by the back of the neck and tossed it gracefully over her head; a click sound signalled a broken neck. With the dead rat in her mouth, she made her way quickly upstairs, in a hurry it seemed, to finish the job.

In 1938 or 1939, only a few years after our ground-breaking party for Harold Sumberg and his bride, some unfortunates of meager intelligence painted an enormous swastika in black on Rabbi and Mrs Eisendrath's beautiful yellow front door. It was such a pretty house, not ostentatious, all white, with that golden-yellow door as an accent. It was a showplace in Moore Park, on the corner of MacClelland Road and Inglewood Drive.

How much attitudes had changed in just a few years became clear when someone approached Mother to phone Mrs Eisendrath the morning after the disgraceful event. Home from school for lunch, I overheard Mother begging the rabbi's wife not to let anyone touch the door during the day. Before supper that evening, a crowd of neighbours arrived at the Eisendraths' door carrying brushes and a large can of yellow paint. The men – stockbrokers, lawyers, doctors, teachers (it was Friday, so Dad had to miss it) – all stepped up one by one to make a ceremonial swipe of yellow paint and blot out that odious black sign. There was a sense of seriousness and solidarity, and I do think the rabbi felt genuine surprise. His wife had kept the secret well. The following day painters arrived to do a professional job, but the swastika had already disappeared under yellow paint. Sometimes a foolish action can have a far-reaching and positive effect.

Every once in a while, a soloist with the Toronto Symphony Orchestra or a Proms concert would come to our home for dinner, usually after the rehearsal and the night before the performance. So too, friends of Dad's from his travels or really old friends of Mother and Dad's from their London days would join us. On one such evening, it was a cellist who came to dine. He had been to the house several times before, and I had the merriest memories of his electing to sit on the floor in front of the fire. His legs were so long that it was, he said, the most comfortable position for him, and I usually sat beside him, also stretching my legs out in front.

This last time he came to dinner when I was still at home must have been in the mid-1930s. I seem to remember that the recent burning of books in Leipzig had appalled us, as had German relatives of friends informing us that the destruction had affected only really pornographic books – Hitler had just ordered a cleansing of unpleasant material from the libraries. But who is to say which books are pornographic and what sort of library handles pornography and whose opinion decided on which book? It was a loaded question that bothered me.

At one point at dinner, Dad asked our guest how his brother was. Suddenly it seemed as though the room had chilled and it really felt cold. Our guest's voice was so low that we could hardly hear him. He told us that the Gestapo had seized his brother, the concertmaster of an orchestra in Germany, in the middle of the night. Authorities tossed him into prison with no charges and no visit from a lawyer. He pleaded with a guard to let him have his violin so that he could at least keep his practice normal. The guards poured concentrated sulphuric acid on his fingertips. Then they gave him a violin, and in atrocious pain he went completely mad. They either shot him in the prison or sent him to a concentration camp – his brother did not know. It seemed to me that this was completely evil and that there would be war. Such treatment of a helpless and blameless human being had to stop.

When we heard again at school that the Nazis had burned only bad books, I didn't buy it. One day we saw on a news reel British Prime Minister Neville Chamberlain descending from a plane waving a piece of paper and telling the world that Hitler had assured him that all was serene and that war was not on the agenda. This disgusting sight dumbfounded me. That the British leader could be such an innocent ninny was profoundly troubling. I thought of the members of our provincial legislature behaving like undisciplined school bullies that day when Peggy and I visited. The Speaker had just walked out, but how could we walk out on this abomination? We couldn't, and we didn't, and six years of war altered our lives.

PART IV

Great Honours and Invisible Stitches

CHAPTER ELEVEN

War Years

Everyone tried to do their bit. In any crowded streetcar in Toronto, people looked down on a woman without her knitting bag and a warm balaclava or a wool sock on the way. Bunny, my middle brother, joined the Queen's Own Rifles. His battalion was dispatched to Newfoundland, where the men frequently sighted German U-boats. The army was in such a hurry to ship the battalion off to war that it had no pajamas for the men. The women of the Queen's Own Rifles chapter of the Imperial Order Daughters of the Empire took over the Sunday School room of Christ Church, Deer Park. We all cut and sewed flannelette pajamas as fast as we could. Somebody told me to sit at a donated sewing machine and await instructions. An older woman taught me to stitch a fly in pajama pants, and that's what I did all day long for almost a week. We finished the job in time to send our Queen's Own boys off with two pairs of pajamas each.

The morning that papers showed the desolation of Coventry, England, after its bombardment in November 1940, Dad made an announcement to us at the breakfast table. The Royal Canadian College of Organists (RCCO), of which he was president, would start fund-raising organ recitals for a new organ for Coventry Cathedral, with a target of £10,000. These events continued through the next five years, and eventually the college presented the cathedral with a cheque a little over the target – actually two-fifths of the cost of the new organ. Dad received one of the 24 crucifixes that craftspeople had made from two ancient nails that workers recovered from the ruins of the roof, and he passed it on to St Mary Magdalene's, where it now hangs on a pillar. The only other Coventry crucifix that I have ever seen is on the ruined wall of the church in Berlin where German emperors were crowned, which the British bombed in the Great War.

When Dad told us about his plans for the RCCO, what struck me was his instantaneous decision to help prepare for peace and victory. To him it was an outrage that the Germans could raze a beautiful old monument like that, not to mention the horrendous loss of life and property. We were only beginning to realize late that November that there would be other horrors in the war and that one had to steel oneself to what seemed unbearably shocking.

Not long after Coventry, during the Battle of Britain, Mother received a letter from her eldest brother, Jack Hall, whom we had visited in 1926. Uncle Jack was a fire warden, perching himself on a roof with a pair of binoculars and reporting any fires after a bomb had hit. He had been playing his violin in a performance at the Crystal Palace as usual and had been looking forward to a cup of tea and bed in his own home after the nightlong watch. Unfortunately, the Halls' side of Upper Norwood took a hit that demolished their half of the street, and Aunt Jessie with it. The other side of the street was unscathed. As he couldn't see Upper Norwood from his perch, he had had no idea that he was now homeless and a widower until he reached his address. He wrote to Mother that he was so thankful that he hadn't dropped off his precious violin at home before reporting for fire duty. It was now his one and only possession. My cousin Leslie was in North Africa, part of the force taking on Rommel, and Madeleine was doing war work elsewhere.

Mr Saunders, still our milkman, had a new story for Mother. He had joined up in a Home Defence Brigade, which posted him to guard the reservoir pond at Avoca Avenue and Rosehill Avenue, east of Yonge Street and south of St Clair. The pond and the park were the source of drinking water for people who lived above the St Clair hill. He bore a wooden replica of a rifle!

The previous night, he told Mother, he had seen a man prowling around the raised, open, circular pond, which had a gravelled promenade around it and was a popular spot for neighbours to walk on Sunday afternoons with well-behaved dogs. Mr Saunders challenged the man – two or three in the morning is not a usual time for a stroll. The fellow replied that he was looking for mushrooms. On a gravel path? Hardly, thought Mr Saunders. The rifle was of course no good for shooting, so instead he whacked the character on the head with it.

The policeman on duty happened along at the right moment. The two overpowered the fellow and searched him. They found a supply of cyanide, enough to put all of us in the area out of business for good. Barbed wire appeared without delay, and authorities covered over our pond, our reservoir. Saunders received a real rifle – a Great War relic, he told Mother.

Mother, Dad, and I all went to the same hairdresser, the Cecil Gill Salon, a one-man show, with a studio on Yonge Street south of St Clair. Cecil Gill knew his business. He had apprenticed at Louis and Bernard, the court hairdressers in London and, after years of lowly jobs, had risen to accompanying a senior hairdresser every morning to Buckingham Palace, where he had held the pins that his senior tucked into Queen Mary's hair. Everyone whom we knew went to his salon. He gave Mother a marcel wave every week. And he thinned out my over-abundant thatch every two weeks. Every two or three weeks, Dad used to remark to the world in general, "I must get a haircut, or somebody will mistake me for a musician, a typically frowsy-headed one."

As many Londoners in Toronto seemed to do, Mr Gill confided in Mother. He told her of the young woman to whom he had proposed and who had accepted him. She then broke off the engagement, sued him for breach of promise, and kept the diamond ring that he had given her. To assuage his grief and anger at allowing such a gold digger to delude him, he saved up his gas rationing coupons and took off for a solo weekend in Montreal. Before the days of the 401, No. 2 Highway was the way to go, and, being very old, it hugged the shoreline of Lake Ontario and the St Lawrence River. Photography was Mr Gill's hobby; he was always at the ready for a good shot, and his camera sat beside him in the car.

Somewhere very near Kingston, he was enjoying the scenery and in particular an immense old wooden barn right at water's edge. After studying it briefly, he concluded that there was something odd about it and slowed down for a longer look. It had the customary lightning arrester on the roof, but he thought that there was an unusual amount of hardware as well. He snapped the picturesque barn and made a note of its location.

When he had his pictures developed, he showed Mother a print of the barn, and it did have what seemed to be an inordinate number, a platoon, of lightning arresters. What should he do? he asked Mother. Mother took the print home and showed it to Dad. My father looked at the snap, "h'mm"ed for a while, and then decided to contact the boss of one of his sopranos in St Mary's choir, a senior officer of the Royal Canadian Mounted Police (RCMP) in Toronto.

That picture created a stir indeed. The RCMP official, a Mr King, immediately asked for the negative and the exact location of the barn. Eventually word came back from him. Even though the 'Mounties' were well aware that sources were picking up information about movement of ship convoys and relaying it to German submarines, they had not been able to pinpoint the leak. And here it was in black and white from an alert and observant tourist. We all felt that Mr Gill should have received some sort of citation, for he must have prevented the loss of scores of ships and all the lives on board, not to mention food and war materiel for desperate Britain.

As members of the Women's Division (WDs) of the Royal Canadian Air Force (RCAF) paraded in Queen's Park one Sunday afternoon, Cecil Gill was there with his camera. He noted with disgust the varying hair styles of the young women, some with hair flopping over their collars, some with hair curled up in readiness for a party but not, in his opinion, suitable to go with a smart, well-cut blue uniform. He snapped several pictures and took them down to RCAF Headquarters, pointing out how impressive the women looked from their shoulders to their well-shone shoes. Their hair could look much better, he felt. He closed his salon for the duration and went off to war. After he returned, he reopened it on Bloor Street, much more trendy, but not nearly so neighbourly, even though his artistry was certainly more than equal to its upscale neighbours.

Morning after morning at home, we woke up to the sound of a corvette down in the harbour making the sounds that it produces when it is undergoing testing for service: three notes – middle C, then F, then D prime – quite distinctive. It probably hooted at other times, but it was in the quiet of early morning, just waking up, that we were aware of the sound.

CHAPTER TWELVE

Golden Years

The only time that I ever remember Dad's being bitter was one day just after his retirement in 1950. The usual age for stepping down was 65, but the University of Toronto had kept him on an extra five years. His *Cap and Gown Magazine* had just arrived, and it contained the university's advertisement for a replacement for his position at twice his salary. That made him angry and disgusted him. He told me the niggardly sum that he had been receiving, and it shocked me. It was considerably less than the starting salary of a kindergarten teacher. Is it any wonder many Canadian graduates have gone to teach elsewhere?

Having reached the biblical three score and ten in 1950, Dad went to see our family physician, Uncle Harold Ball, for a complete overhaul. Lately he thought that he had been feeling a little more tired than usual. From going upstairs – leaping up the steps three at a time – he had started to take them only two at a time. Did he perhaps need some kind of tonic? Uncle Harold asked him to run down an average day's activities. By the time Dad reached a break for a cup of tea around four o'clock, the doctor said, "Stop! Stop! I'm exhausted just listening to you. I couldn't begin to keep up with your schedule."

In the period around Dad's retirement, so much was happening. Dad had finally found time to rework and revise Symphony No. 2, and the first performance was to take place May 18, 1950, in Massey Hall, with Ettore Mazzoleni conducting the Royal Conservatory of Music orchestra.

Hugh Davidson, the young music critic of the *Toronto Daily Star*, opined that a major work such as this, coming after the successful première of Symphony No. 1, should receive a public performance by the Toronto Symphony Orchestra. Eight years later, he still believed that Toronto had waited far too long for such an event. The *Star* then sponsored the orchestra's concert, under the baton of Walter Susskind, its new conductor. Dad appreciated the attention that Susskind had given to the score and to the performance. As usual, he took his bows to a standing ovation wearing his favourite black velvet jacket. Nothing that Mother could say would convince him to wear the customary white tie and tails, which he always referred to as a 'monkey suit' and thought quite ridiculous.

Hugh Davidson and his wife, Joan, were neighbours of my parents. During casual conversations, sometimes on the street, occasionally in a grocery shop, he discovered Mother's musical background. In frequent phone calls to her, he set about expanding his understanding of his new posting and sharpening his perception of matters musical. Mother thoroughly enjoyed his attention. After one of his early assignments, reviewing a performance of Handel's *Messiah*, he phoned Mother, telling her in a breathless outpouring how affecting the oratorio was and how at the end of part II, just before its closing chorus, the whole audience rose spontaneously to its feet.

Mother gently brought him back to ground and told him about the custom of people standing for the Hallelujah Chorus, ever since King George II, attending an early performance in London, allegedly rose and stood until the end of the chorus. So everybody else in the audience had to stand up too. This tradition has persisted, despite wits who proclaim that His Majesty was dozing and the opening of the Hallelujah Chorus startled him awake and up on his feet. Hugh Davidson called Mother frequently after that. She had saved him from a gaffe, from becoming a real laughing stock. She enjoyed his and Joan's company, and they had many a cup of tea together, particularly just before he was off to his reviewing duties.

Our parents had always lived frugally, partly from necessity, partly from taste. When Dad's retirement from the university was really approaching, it hit home to them both that his university pension would equal half of his salary at retirement, giving him a new impetus to 'publish or perish.' Otherwise they would be living below the poverty line.

Mother's first reaction, really in a panic, was to think of selling 139 and looking for something smaller in the neighbourhood – a reasonable idea, as the brothers and I had all decamped. I had married in 1943. Without a word to Dad, Mother started looking for smaller quarters within the new budget and asked me to go with her. It was dreadful, only cramped little duplexes, and how could that work with Dad composing at all hours on the piano? Mother felt really sad. Dad was gaining more recognition than ever as a composer in Britain, continental Europe, and the United States, but how to get by?

Harold Moon of Broadcast Music Incorporated (BMI) came to the rescue. He introduced Dad to Ed Klammer of Concordia Publishing in St Louis, Missouri. Mr Klammer commissioned Dad to write the anthem that his firm had been seeking to start the Sunday services of the Southern Conference of the Lutheran Church. Dad set the words of *Sing to the Lord of Harvest*, and every U.S. Lutheran church used it, including those in the Northern Conference. The royalty cheques came pouring in for the rest of their lives and beyond. Money was no longer a problem.

A meeting earlier in 1952 made a significant difference in Dad's life. The Royal School of Church Music in London had changed practice over the years from holding examinations and influencing organists' choices of music across Canada to concentrating on only three cities, Toronto, Montreal, and Kingston. Dad chaired the meeting to figure out what to do to increase interest in the Royal School. The guest of honour was William McKie, the school's director and organist of Westminster Abbey. The two men became good friends immediately.

The same year Dad learned of the selection of his *An Apostrophe to the Heavenly Hosts* (1921) for performance at London's annual St Cecilia's Day concert – the saint's day is November 22. It was the first work by a 'Dominion' composer to grace the event – a benefit for the Musicians Benevolent Fund. The Queen and the Duke of Edinburgh were present. Dad met the sovereign and reported at home that the ovation for *Apostrophe* pleased him. *The Times* called it "a surprise from Canada." Mother retorted, "Do they think we all wear moccasins and go about in canoes?" The sponsors asked for another anthem from him for the next year's concert.

On the same visit, William McKie asked Dad to write an homage anthem for the coronation of the new queen on June 2, 1953, and there was no time to lose. The morning after the St Cecilia's Day concert, he went straight to the library of the Savage Club, an affiliate of the Arts and Letters, where he was staying. There he spotted an aged prayer book containing a service of thanksgiving for the long reign of Queen Victoria. It contained a selection of verses from various psalms. Dad knew that book of the Old Testament almost by heart anyway. He rearranged the excerpts, added some bits, and sent his selection off to William in haste. The archbishop of Canterbury gave his approval the same evening.

Dad could indeed pick out verses and knew which psalm they belonged to. When I was at St Mildred's, the standard punishment for our rather mild schoolgirl antics was learning a psalm. I complained about this to Dad one evening when I was struggling with one of them. In no uncertain terms he informed me that I was memorizing some of the finest poetry extant and that it was a privilege. I didn't agree, but I held my counsel. I soon came to realize, however, in Dora

Mavor Moore's classes that learning psalms made learning lines in a play much easier. For a more serious misdemeanour, I had to write out the definition of the word 'civilized' in the *Oxford English Dictionary* 100 times. That is one text that I have never forgotten.

So Dad returned from London with his work for 1953 cut out – two anthems for state occasions in London, works for important broadcasts and events in Canada, and a few other contracts awaiting his attention. He always seemed happiest when working at full speed to a strict deadline. When he arrived home from London he was eager to start right to work.

As we saw above, Burke's *Chronicle of the Landed Gentry* asked Dad for information on the Canadian Willans for its coronation version. That request went straight to the waste-paper basket. Inclusion cost a modest sum, and Dad exploded. Mother agreed.

It was the first time a non-resident had composed music for a British coronation. In the ceremony, Dad's homage anthem, *O Lord, Our Governour,* was first among anthems as the peers of the realm made their obeisance to the Queen, starting with her duke. Dad was at the service, but not Mother: she would have so enjoyed it, but she felt that they could not afford it – they could not stretch the budget that far. Their sometime neighbours Louis and Sara Breithaupt were there; they had rented the house across the street after he became lieutenant-governor in early 1952, and whenever snow started falling ploughs appeared on Inglewood almost instantly, as if by magic.

From his 70s on, Dad received a number of distinctions, including several honorary LLDs and DLitts. When yet another one rolled in, Mother remarked quietly that the honorary part was pleasant indeed, but it wasn't going to help the eaves-troughs, which were overdue for replacement. One honour that Dad especially cherished was the Lambeth Degree of Doctor of Music. The archbishop of Canterbury bestows it in the name of the Church of England, and it has a high ranking in precedence when academics form up in a procession.

Dad was to have received it in February 1956, but worrisome heart attacks forced a postponement for six months.

What with that delay and the deterioration in health of Ralph Vaughan Williams, the two men never did meet. Vaughan Williams wrote to Dad to tell him of his great disappointment at not being fit enough to attend the Lambeth ceremony in July. After many years of exchanging cards on their mutual birthday, October 12, and corresponding on various musical matters, both felt the disappointment keenly.

Dad's friend William McKie played the organ at the ceremony in London, and so another academic gown and hood joined the array in the big box in my parents' linen cupboard. One way the neighbours could tell it was convocation time again every June was by the brilliant gowns and hoods that Mother pinned out on the clothesline in our garden for a good freshening. They eventually made quite an imposing lineup. We also knew that summer was approaching when Mother hung Dad's summer jacket, white flannel, out on the line. It was becoming really old and yellow. Mother asked him for years and years to see about a new one, but he loved the antique, and that was that.

William McKie's wedding in 1956 saw the première of another of my father's compositions in Westminster Abbey. Now Sir William, he married Barbara Birks of the Canadian jewellery family. Dad's wedding gift to them was *Epithalame*, to send them out of the great church after the ceremony on a high note of celebration. Dad was unable to be present.

In the midst of all the commissions, performances, and broadcasts, at a ceremony at city hall on a Friday in Toronto, Mayor Nathan Phillips bestowed on Dad an award of merit. Dad left the reception to attend choir practice, and the mayor's wife asked Mother how she was travelling home. Bus and the new subway were her usual means of transport, but Mrs Phillips wouldn't hear of such a thing.

She would take Mother home in the mayor's official limousine if she didn't mind waiting until the reception ended. Mother thanked her and prepared to wait.

Finally His Worship and his spouse were ready to set off. Mrs Phillips caught sight of a big platter of lobster sandwiches that guests had hardly touched. She insisted that Mother take some home with her and wrapped a couple of dozen in a number of paper napkins. She asked for something to put them in, Mother meanwhile trying to turn down the offer. The mayor's wife insisted, and someone produced a brown paper bag. As soon as Mrs Phillips handed the bag to her, Mother realized with horror that the bag was leaving a trail of lobsterish juice across the lobby.

Her hostess had paid no attention. Mother told me the next day, when her embarrassment had passed and she could laugh about it, that she must have left a ghastly mess on the carpet in the official limousine. I suggested that she not worry. It was more than possible that the chauffeur had cleaned up the car after Mrs Phillips went home with goodies from other parties too. Everyone enjoys snacking on the leftovers after the guests have departed. Mother offered me a lobster sandwich, "But eat it here. They leak."

By the 1950s, magazines and newspapers with articles on my father or interviews with him seemed to arrive every week, even more often. Dad was becoming a celebrity, so much so that tour buses would come along Inglewood Drive and pause at 139. All heads would turn together sharply to have a look. Tommy, Mother's handyman and gardener, was often doing something about the place and got a tremendous kick out of his almost-celebrity status. Sometimes Mother and I did a little gardening together, trying to discourage the Virginia creeper from blocking windows, trimming the lilac bushes, and tidying the hollyhocks that had taken over our driveway since there was no car using it. "Just ignore the sightseers," Mother told me, but you had to wonder what the busload of gawkers was learning about us.

A large carton of dishes, various bits and pieces that Mother decided to clear out, was sitting in the back hall one day. The contents were for pickup for a yard sale by the Toronto Humane Society. They included the tea and coffee set that St Paul's had presented to Dad when he left the church some forty and more years earlier – a Rogers silver-plated teapot, coffee pot, cream jug, and sugar bowl. Mother never liked it. Where she came from, a presentation of silver had to be sterling, and she had always turned up her nose at the set – another instance of Mother and Toronto's standards differing. She had used it only when her silver teapot needed an accomplice. I asked her if I could rescue it, and I picked up the distinct impression that my tastes were not 'up to snuff.' But I carried the pieces home, and the engraved "H.W." is the good part for me. Sorry about that, Humane Society. But when Mother died in 1964, the brothers and I, with Dad's approval, requested that we would appreciate, instead of flowers, donations to the Humane Society. Its people told us that they had never had such an avalanche for one person's memorial.

Broadcast Music Incorporated, or BMI, in New York logs performances and collects fees for composers and wanted to establish itself in Canada as well. Dad had much more income from American publishers and performances. Harold Moon of BMI, who had put my father in contact with Ed Klammer of Concordia Publishing, visited Toronto to persuade Dad to become its first Canadian affiliate; others would follow, he reasoned, and they did.

Harold Moon and Dad became great pals. At one point they had travelled together for a few days and discovered a mutual and conflicting interest in Shakespeare. Dad was sure that the playwright had written his own stuff, and Mr Moon credited the Earl of Essex. They disagreed happily, bickering back and forth for years.

For Dad's 75th birthday in 1955, Harold Moon gave him three first editions: Shakespeare's *King John*, probably the prompter's copy from the Globe Theatre; the *Collected Works of Ben Jonson*; and an apparent first edition of Bacon's *Essays*. Dad let me read them, with clean hands and great care.

Midmorning on my father's 80th, Harold Moon arrived with 80 bottles of wine, spirits, and liqueurs in decorated cartons, piling the living-room high with birthday loot. My parents drank very little but enjoyed the odd glass. Seven years later, after Dad's death, we saw how many of the 80 bottles there still were in the cellar, and I know that Dad had given away several.

In 1959, the National Film Board's music director, Robert Fleming – he of the one-minute Christmas Eve operas at 139 – delegated another former student of my father's, Louis Applebaum, to be music supervisor of a 17-minute short, *Man of Music,* about Dad. Robert Blais produced it, and he and Dad formed a mutual admiration, each working long hours and staying light-hearted often until four in the morning and then going at it again next day at the regular starting time. The schedule was as inconvenient as a movie's usually is. A lot of the filming took place at St Mary Magdalene's at ungodly hours, when the noise of passing traffic was at a minimum. Even for a person of such robust health as my father it was tiring at 79, and he had a heart attack after filming ended.

Mother had a minor role, her movie initiation. Her action was to knock on the study door holding a tea tray, peer around the door, and utter the deathless line, "Are you ready for tea, Healey?" For the first take, Mother made a pot of tea, arranged the tray, cosy and all, and carried it from the kitchen to the stairs, up the stairs, and across the hall, ready to knock on the door at the director's cue. On the first take she was perfect. But of course there was a second. Mother went downstairs and brewed a fresh pot, repeating her trek up to the set.

There were 32 takes in all. Robert wanted different lighting, someone reloaded the camera, and on and on. Mother was flawless each take. Nobody thought to tell her that there was no need for a fresh pot of tea, no need to go downstairs every time, no need to do anything but find a seat until the 'techies' were ready for her. After the 31st take, she had had enough and was so angry that she was ready to blow up. She emptied the pot to prepare for a fresh brew of wasted effort and nearly threw the teapot at the wall.

Mother and Dad's dog, Trixie, must have watched the whole affair. She stood up slowly, caught Mother's attention, and winked. Mother broke up laughing, and at the next take, the 32nd, when the director announced that he was satisfied, Mother, in her sweetest tone, told him that he was a very lucky man. One more take, she told him, and she had been planning to pour the entire pot of hot tea right on top of his head. There was general laughter, and then Robert and his crew realized that she had overdone the realism, and everybody apologized. But as she told me, "Trixie saved the day with that wink."

A lively friend and former pupil, Horace Lapp, enlivened my parents' later years. Horace was always fun to be with, possessing a constant smile that showed a mouthful of big teeth. No matter what happened, he always laughed with infectious merriment. He and Dad made quite a pair. Horace had a weakness for Maynard's Made in View chocolates. He could be going full tilt down any busy street, but a Maynard's sign would bring his car to a squealing halt, and he and Dad would rush in for a chocolate splurge. How he managed it, we don't know, but he never received a ticket.

Horace was always good for a funny tale of the silent-movie days, when he had interpreted the action on screen on an enormous pipe organ. There had been two stellar performers creating sound tracks for the 'silents' in Toronto: Kate Smith and Horace Lapp. The biggest organ was in a theatre, Shea's, where the foreground of the 'new' city hall now stands. Horace possessed a vast repertoire, knowing key signatures as well as appropriate melodies, ranging from what he called "umpity bump stuff" to the romantic, as the stars of the silents gazed rapturously into each other's eyes and the Hayes Office timed their kisses. This might well immediately follow something quite hair raising. Horace had some near-disasters when he had to push and pull organ stops, change gears mentally with no warning, and keep an eye on the screen.

When Horace was coming for tea, Mother always set out a plateful of Pantry Cookies, crisp, gingery biscuits, and the plate always emptied. Aside from Made in View chocolates, Pantry Cookies was his other passion. With his natural high spirits, he frequently entertained in an organ program illustrating the role of the movie organist. One time he was organizing a big public concert, preparing to adapt various up-to-date Broadway hits into what might have worked in a particular silent. Dad was apprehensive. He tried to help his friend to recognize that he was in fact arranging copyright material without permission, which was asking for trouble. Horace appeared to listen but would not budge. That no one sued him had Dad shaking his head. Horace always seemed to have some kind of immunity to trouble.

When Waterloo Music wanted to put some of Dad's early songs back into print, Horace Lapp and Dad went off to Waterloo together on many a jaunt. It seemed to be more of an outing than a business trip. After their excursions, like two truant school kids, they brought what remained of their manhandled chocolates to present to Mother, who then put the kettle on and sorted out the Pantry Cookies. It became a ritual.

Although Mother bought those special cookies for her frequent tea guest, she was a self-taught cook well ahead of her time. White bread was only for invalids; white sugar was only for tea. Brown bread, whole-wheat flour, raw sugar, and no carbonated drinks were standard practice in her kitchen. As a young man in London, Dad had apparently suffered from kidney stones. A Harley Street specialist advised him to cut out anything fried, re-cooked meat, and pies. Mother adhered to this advice religiously. She probably knew that Dad regularly had a Friday supper of fried bacon and eggs at Murray's Restaurant on Bloor Street at Avenue Road. The eatery was almost on his way from the music faculty to choir practice. Mother would just sigh, with a "What can I do with that man?" look on her face. 'No carbonated drinks' was an injunction from her childhood. Apparently a friend of Grandfather Hall's owned a company that made 'squash'; he told Grandfather that, although it was a great business, he should never allow his children to drink the stuff. So her children didn't drink it either.

The morning after Mother's death in December 1964, when I arrived on the first plane to Toronto from New York where I was living, I searched for a clean shirt for him. I found his shirts in the ironing basket, all veterans well past praying for, favourites that he could not bring himself to throw out. So Mother had turned the collars and cuffs with stitches so tiny that they would have been acceptable even to plutocratic ladies of medieval Paris. Such painstaking care made me want to cry. How long it must have taken her to make such virtually invisible stitches. You have to love a person a very great deal to do that much just to prolong the life of a beloved shirt.

The same night, after everyone had gone home, Dad and I went up to his study, his 'junk room' he called it, because he chucked everything musical in there somewhere. We were just going over the day's events quietly when suddenly he jumped up, went to the piano, and began to play. He must have played non-stop for at least half an hour. It was music that I had never heard before, and it was transcendentally lovely, ethereal. I asked him what it was, and he said very quietly, with his head bowed, "I was just thinking of your Mother." At last I understood: for all their seeming aloofness to each other at times, and always in public, they simply adored each other.

The centennial of Canada's Confederation led to a yearlong celebration in 1967. That year too, Roland Michener succeeded Governor General Georges Vanier, who died in office. Uncle Roly and, I believe, Aunt Norah were instrumental in establishing the Order of Canada for distinguished citizens. The first investiture was in November 1967, and Dad became a companion of the new order, the highest level of three. He asked me to accompany him to Ottawa, but his cataracts had worsened, and he was becoming frailer than we realized.

He was still busy writing, however, and in answer to Walter Hinrichsen's request for more hymn anthems, he sent off the latest, *At the Close of the Day*. We had no idea how apt that title was. It was his last work to appear before his death, for C.F. Peters in New York, although he continued to work on his opera, *Deirdre*, scoring the orchestral parts for Berandol Publishers.

After Mother's death, we arranged for Dad a series of housekeepers, hard-to-find people. The best was Lottie, a motherly soul originally from one of the Caribbean islands. She up and left one day in a huff. I found out later that one of the choir girls wanting to make Dad some sort of special dinner had rather taken over the kitchen, Lottie's domain, and no one was going to elbow Lottie out of her kitchen. She knew what Dad liked to eat, and she had made preparations for dinner. Finding another housekeeper to equal her was a thankless task, but we soon needed a live-in practical nurse.

It was my habit to visit 139 from Oakville, where I was living, a few days each week, and Dad and I had a special time together, just talking and reminiscing. Dad told me tales of his young days in London. He and his special chum, Bunny Green – a medical student who died in the South African, or Boer War – a couple of young blades around town it seemed, both loved music performances, a major expense for them, so they were always up in 'the gods,' or the 'nosebleed' sections. Dad told me of their going to a symphony concert in the Royal Albert Hall, capacity 8,000. Serge Koussevitzky played in the double-bass section; he later became the longtime conductor of the Boston Symphony. At some point Koussevitzky, a very tall man playing a very big instrument, made an entry inadvertently on a falsetto. The high-pitched screech coming out of all that mass of man and fiddle set Dad and Bunny off. They giggled, chortled, and finally roared uncontrollably. An usher arrived and escorted them out of the hall. Dad told me that they were still laughing hysterically all the way to the Cromwell Road.

I then told Dad about being in a small bar in the West 40s in New York to hear a well-known double-bassist. After a while it was obvious that Koussevitzky's daughter was sitting next to me in the crowded bar, and we started chatting, filling in for each other our fathers' lives as young musicians in London. As is usual with musicians and, it seems, with their daughters as well, we were in the bar long after closing time, with the double-bass player extemporizing on themes both jazz and classical. He was familiar with the names of both our fathers and appeared to be having as much fun as we were.

Dad reminisced one time about E. Power Biggs, a young English organist with large ambitions who had just arrived in Toronto and sought his advice. Biggs told Dad that he really wanted to be a concert organist – how could he become one? Dad told me that he gave the young man a detailed schedule, which he followed to the letter. He advised Biggs to leave Canada and find a job as a church organist in an Episcopalian church outside New York City. He should make certain that the church was in an affluent community, a suburb for executives. He should practise diligently every day for at least two years before even thinking of giving organ recitals. Then when he thought himself ready, he should go to it. A reputation as a fine young organist would set him on his way.

Biggs followed Dad's instructions, became a celebrated concert performer, and even became the subject of a little poem in the *New Yorker*, starting off, "More E. Power to you Biggs." He fulfilled his ambition to play on every organ in Germany on which J.S. Bach had played and made numerous recordings. He once performed in Hamilton, Ontario, in the same church where Dora Mavor Moore had presented *Everyman*. As the art, music, and drama critic on the *Hamilton Spectator* at the time, I went to interview him prior to the recital. We had a great time, and I obtained the story. Then I had to file a review. The city editor wanted to chop my story into something so small that it would be hard to find. I growled at him and pointed out a few salient facts. The crowd had absolutely jammed the church, there were extra chairs everywhere, a crowd of standees filled the narthex, and some people stood out in the street. Thank goodness the fire marshal hadn't shown up. The Hamilton Tiger Cats football team would have been proud to have such a large and enthusiastic crowd. The review appeared as I had written it.

Dad and I often talked about opera. He was deeply in love with his *Deirdre*, and every so often he would go to the piano to make a point. He also asked me again to accompany him to London for a Ring Cycle, something that he had wanted to do all his life, he said. I don't think that Mother would have been so keen. She was a fan more of Brahms than of Wagner. Brahms was her *second*-favourite composer. In her young days, Brahms and Wagner fans were apt to be of stridently differing opinions. Of course I agreed with his suggestion, but I knew that he would find it an exhausting experience. Perhaps we both realized that it was a pipe dream.

One day, he told me, a young high-school teacher, a member of the St Mary's choir, visited him to ask if he thought it possible to make a living out of conducting a professional choir. The memory still made Dad chuckle. There were no professional choirs in Canada at the time, and very few in the United States. Dad gave him substantially the same advice that he had given E. Power Biggs. Find a small group of like-minded singers and practise, practise, practise without giving up your day job.

Elmer Iseler took Dad's advice to heart, and his choir made a debut in Stratford in 1955 as the Festival Choir with Dad's *Song of Welcome* to inaugurate a music season to accompany Shakespeare's plays. There was a big party afterwards on the second floor of a Chinese restaurant on the city's main square – a jolly occasion. The troupe toured Canada and the world and later became the Elmer Iseler Singers. After Elmer's death, Lydia Adams took over. The company under Lydia is still a top-rated professional choir.

Reminiscing again about opera and Bunny Green and his escapades in London, Dad told me about a *Tristan und Isolde* that they saw at Covent Garden. Again they were up in the cheap seats. In the second act there is a love duet, an extended love duet in fact. Isolde sat on a bench and shifted a bit towards the end of the bench after about twenty minutes of their protestations of passion. Tristan put his foot on the very edge of the bench, probably as he had done in rehearsal, but Isolde, a hefty Wagnerian soprano, had not wriggled towards the end. The bench upended, and Isolde landed flat out on top of Tristan, who landed on his back. It was an appropriate position for the two declaiming their passion for one another, but it brought the house down. The youthful pair in the gods laughed so hard and so long, even after the orchestra had carried on bravely, that ushers asked them to leave.

"That's twice you were thrown out of a performance?" I asked.

"Yes, but it was worth it both times," Dad smiled, still laughing at the memory.

After a day of delightful gossiping and sharing memories with Dad, I used to drive home to Oakville via Avenue Road and park outside the Secrett Jewel Salon. I knew Vic Secrett, and his sister Mary went to Havergal College with me. Of course Dad knew their father, the rector at the Church of the Redeemer opposite Vic's salon.

"Why do I drop in like this?" I asked Vic. "I am not in a position to buy anything, but I do feel an urge to look at these stones."

"You are witnessing the passing of a human life," he told me, "and you want to be assured that some things, like these beautiful, natural stones, last forever. You know you are welcome."

In the 1960s it was possible to drive down Avenue Road, pull into the curb, and just leave the car – no restrictions, no parking tickets, sometimes not even bothering to lock up.

After a couple of heart attacks and playing his final Christmas Eve service in 1967, on what must have been automatic pilot, Dad began the cataract operations. It was much more complicated then than now. He was unable to see anything and was in a gloomy hospital room in the Wellesley Hospital. He was there for some days. The room appalled me, as did the view from the window – a brick wall. No wonder the room was gloomy, but perhaps the hospital authorities thought that it didn't matter to a patient who could not see clearly anyway. The brothers and I made a pact not to mention to Dad that an old friend from Hart House days, Vincent Massey, the first Canadian-born governor general, had died. We wanted only happy news for him.

I promised Dad that I would spring him out of this prison and obtained permission to take him home. We placed a hospital bed in his beloved junk room, and he seemed much more serene and content. More heart attacks followed.

One night it was too painful for him to lie down, so all night long he sat in his favourite chair. I perched on its arm and massaged his back. He talked to me about Grandmother Willan and her sense of fun. He talked about the afternoon he went down from London to Bexhill to see her, as she wasn't well. In the course of conversation, he asked her what she would like to do that evening. With her wonderful, twinkling-eyed smile, she suggested, "Let's go out and fight a policeman." Even in pain, Dad could laugh about her indomitable sense of humour.

Eventually we both watched the sun come up. The day nurse soon arrived, and I went for some rest. About midmorning Dad was back in bed and apparently no longer in pain. I checked to see how he was and took his hand. He took in a little breath, let out a bigger breath, and that was it. I closed his eyes and kissed his forehead and then ran to the window and flung it open all the way on a cold February morning. I wondered for years why I had done such a thing.

In the crowded funeral home, it sounded more like an unending cocktail party. Everybody had jokes that they remembered Dad's telling, his limericks, nutty things that they had done with him, apt and witty things that he had said. Jeanette Zarou's father came over and told me how he and Dad shared a love of spats, and the only place that he could buy them latterly was Simpson's – a tip from Dad. The store invited each of them to paw through a big box of unmatched spats and try to pair them without hindrance from salesclerks.

Dora Mavor Moore put me straight on why I opened Dad's window after he died. One evening I had taken a couple of TV dinners to her at the old house on Bathurst Street so that we could have a cosy gossip in front of her fireplace, as had become our custom. She asked me particularly to tell her about Dad's death. I did and asked her why I would open the window in such a frenzy.

She replied firmly, "You're a Celt. You know why you did that. It was instinct. You had to open the window and let the soul fly free."

Postlude: The Music Goes On ...

Aunt Norah Michener asked me, not long after Dad's funeral, if there were portraits of him. Well, yes, there were some sketches, but nothing so formal as a portrait. I have that cartoon of Dad that A.Y. Jackson did for me on the back of the Maurice Cullen catalogue from the exhibit in the Art Gallery of Hamilton. It is a very informal sketch.

Aunt Norah took charge and commissioned J.M. Reynolds to make a bust of Dad. The sculptor asked me for photographs, and I suggested that he model the shape of the skull from my eldest brother, Michael. Walking downstairs behind Michael not long before, I had realized how very similar their heads looked from behind. I don't think that Mr Reynolds ever took me up on that suggestion, and the bust has never entirely pleased me.

He cast four bronzes. One went to the Royal School of Church Music in London, of which Dad had become a Fellow. One is in Canada House in London, and one in Toronto's Roy Thomson Hall. The fourth went on display at the Bluma Appel Theatre in Toronto, along with other Reynolds pieces in a special show of his work, and somebody stole it. William Littler, music critic of the *Toronto Star*, a man with a puckish sense of humour and aware that the bust did not enchant me, accused me of being the thief!

I said, "Sure, Bill. I just picked it up and slung it over my shoulder. Nobody noticed." But it hasn't surfaced yet, to my knowledge.

Various staff people at the Faculty of Music suggested that I just pack the manuscripts into boxes and a University of Toronto truck would pick them up for the faculty archives. Remembering Dad's bitterness and disgust over the much larger salary for his successor in 1950, I refused to consider it and told them so. I repeated my remarks after someone invited me to the university's Rare Book Room to admire the treasures, which included Dad's setting of *The Chester Mysteries*. The thank-you letter that I had come across spelled his name incorrectly as "Healy."

The archive also housed a first edition of Bach's *Preludes and Fugues* with emendations probably in the composer's hand. Another Bach work, an early edition and a treasure, had been on loan to Wanda Landowska for a CBC broadcast. Landowska pencilled in comments here and there and thought that she had a right, as the world's foremost harpsichordist, to keep the book. After the brouhaha died down and she had returned the volume, it emerged that she had scrubbed out her pencil markings with what appeared to be vigorous pressure.

I mentioned to a few musician friends that I had seen the Bach *Preludes and Fugues*, usually under lock and key, and they were all so envious. Section leaders of the Toronto Symphony Orchestra were apparently not important enough to be given a peek.

For a while it looked as though Dad's manuscripts would go offshore. When Aunt Norah Michener, by then in Rideau Hall, asked me what was going to happen with them and I told her of that possibility and others, she declared that they were national treasures and should go to the National Library in Ottawa. She put me in touch with Guy Sylvestre, the institution's director. He was hoping to expand the music holdings and make a Music Section with its own head. Accordingly, Dad's manuscripts found their way to the new Music Section. Three of his books went to the Rare Books Section – the first editions that Harold Moon of BMI gave him for his 75th birthday.

Dad's hoard of Canadian books of poetry is in the library's general collection, along with his extensive range of general reading material. Poets were wont to send him a copy of their latest work in the hope that he might set a poem or two to music.

As it turned out, my experience of having the bedroom above Dad's grand piano from 1935 to 1943 and hearing him work endlessly at his composing proved useful for the National Library. I was able to help Giles Bryant in placing various bits of manuscripts in their proper order for his catalogue of Dad's compositions, on which we worked for the library for a couple of years. I stipulated that the manuscripts should be accessible to anyone with an interest in examining the composer's "own fist," as Giles puts it. I figured that anyone who wants to spend time examining a music manuscript must have a good reason to do so, and I also recalled the anguish of my musical friends at being unable to look at the Bach work in Toronto.

As soon as the National Library announced the acquisition, Mme Champagne, widow of Dad's friend Claude, presented her husband's papers, and promises of others followed. The Music Section has continued to expand and to grow in importance from its start as a few stacks in the library's basement.

Guy Sylvestre asked me if I had suggestions for a suitable head of the Music Section. I said that there was only one person in Canada for the job, Helmut Kallman, who was in charge of the music collection at the CBC. Keith MacMillan, Sir Ernest's son, was on the selection committee, and we agreed that Helmut was the perfect choice.

As soon as the library had sorted my father's papers, Guy organized a gala opening. For the occasion, he arranged padded chairs with built-in sound so that one could sit comfortably and hear Dad's voice in radio interviews and so on – something quite new. He told me that he had always dreamed of a formal opening in the library with the governor general present, and this was his opportunity. Aunt Norah and Uncle Roly Michener were guests of honour, with the Cantata Singers performing a few of Dad's a cappella works. A dinner party followed in the library. I will always remember Guy and Claire Sylvestre, both beaming with pleasure and being such gracious hosts.

I kept learning more about my father's musical sensibilities. He composed hundreds of pieces for services of various church denominations because there was heavy demand right through the first half of the twentieth century. He had a family to feed, and publishers in London, New York, Boston, Germany, and elsewhere just kept sending requests and contracts for items that they wanted.

A musician, a piano teacher I think, told me that, while studying in Vienna and feeling a bit homesick and lost, she walked past a music store and suddenly felt warmth and home. The shop's window displayed Dad's Violin and Piano Sonata No. 2 in E major. Suddenly, she said, home was not so far away after all.

Norman Johnson, a doctoral candidate at the University of Alabama, visited Toronto in the summer of 1970 to study a portion of Dad's manuscripts for his thesis. After we emptied out 139, I stored his manuscripts temporarily, along with his extensive library, in my home in Oakville before they both went to the National Library in Ottawa. Norman stayed a couple of days, and, in comparing Dad's masses – settings of the Christian Eucharist – for three or four denominations, he remarked how perceptive Dad had been and how well he understood the different requirements of each.

Occasionally an event or a chance encounter would remind me of one of my father's disappointments. I attended the National Ballet's *La Prima Ballerina* during the 1967–68 season at Toronto's old O'Keefe Centre – later the Hummingbird and now the Sony Centre. During an intermission, I walked past the work's composer, Godfrey Ridout, sitting in one of those ringside rows down at the front. In the course of conversation, he reported that he had written a fugue into the score for the ballet coming up next on the program. It was a first performance.

"Your Dad would be proud of me, I think. Has anybody ever written a fugue in a ballet before?"

The music was good, and the fugue really worked well, I thought. After the performance, I sweet-talked my way back stage to congratulate the composer. Adoring fans surrounded the National Ballet's Celia Franca, and there was Godfrey, all by himself, looking as though he wished he weren't there. It suddenly hit me: how important it is to go back stage when people whom you know are performing, especially if they are aware that you are in the audience. We made a noisy, celebratory conversation *à deux*. The creator's ego is a fragile thing.

That Celia Franca never asked Dad to compose for one of her ballets was a real disappointment to him. Perhaps she thought that he would make it too liturgical. Perhaps she just didn't realize that he would have loved to write something for her. He was a most loyal fan and in the audience whenever he could spare the time. Perhaps she didn't know that when one of the Adaskins thought that he would write a comedy with music he approached Dad, who agreed to do the music and wrote the overture in no time. Nothing came of the project, but *Overture to an Unwritten Comedy* (1951) was a favourite with orchestras across the country and beyond, although I do not remember the Toronto Symphony Orchestra ever doing it.

I attended a meeting of the American Choral Directors Association in Kansas City in the 1970s as executive director of the Ontario Choral Federation, an arm's-length organization under the provincial government. I sought out the Concordia Publishing booth and thanked Ed Klammer for the security that his publications, particularly of *Sing to the Lord of Harvest*, had given my parents. He said that he had no idea of their situation and ended up in tears. Dad and Ed's children had become real pen pals, exchanging birthday greetings with pleasure. Sometimes Dad wrote little tunes on their cards, he told me.

At the same conference, I was sitting with a few American conductors and Robert Cooper, a brilliant choral and opera conductor, in a bar ankle deep in peanut shells. The conversation turned to Canadian composers, and Bob challenged the Americans to name three. John Beckwith was easy. After a pause, somebody remembered Murray Shafer. Then there was silence. After a decent pause, I asked whether anybody had heard of Willan. At once each of the conductor's said, "Of course." But as one of them added and the rest agreed, "You don't think of Willan as a Canadian any more than you think of Bach as a German. It's just Bach and Willan, no country needed."

Somehow I hope Dad heard that remark. It would please him greatly.

After Dad's death, Leonard Atherton, conductor of the St Catharines Symphony, told me that he was giving a summer-school course in choral conducting at Tanglewood. The study piece was Dad's *Rise Up, My Love,* words of course from the Song of Solomon. Observers from Israel happened to drop in to his lecture and wanted to know where they could obtain this setting of words so familiar to them. So that is how *Rise Up* and now other of my father's works show up regularly on the performance sheets that I receive from SOCAN after use on Israeli radio and TV or in public performance. That too would please Dad.

At the centennial of Dad's birth in 1980, a great service of thanksgiving took place in the Cathedral of St John the Divine in New York. The church dedicated the organ loft to his memory and his music and installed a plaque on the door to the loft. Hundreds of choristers from New York, New Jersey, Ohio, and Pennsylvania sang at the service, filling the chancel of that huge place of worship.

For the service, Dennis Michno, a priest and the organist at All Saints Church on East 54th Street, where I went when I lived in New York, set an orchestral arrangement for some of Dad's motets.

What gave him the idea was the fact that a number of players in the New York Symphony and in the Metropolitan Opera belonged to All Saints, and, as word spread, many orchestral players asked to participate in the celebration. So Dennis wrote something for them to play. He told me that as he was copying out parts for *Rise Up, My Love* he clearly heard a voice commanding him, "Not flutes, trumpets here."

"Did I think … ?" he asked me.

"Yes," I said. "I'm sure of it."

There were various celebrations in 1980 in Canada and in England that I know of, but New York outdid them all. Trumpets it was!

Dad must have made an impression on the young people trying the conservatory's examinations. In the early 1980s, my dear friend Joy Kennedy Clarry, Mary Stewart, and I motored west to see hoodoos, a passion of Joy's. On the way we dropped in to see Joy's cousins throughout the west. Dorothy Hobson of Weyburn asked me to visit a retirement centre. School and music teachers there spoke so lovingly about Dad, even though they had met him only once.

Then I visited the wife of a United Church minister who wanted to meet me. Her parents had been prairie farmers in the difficult 1930s but wanted music for her, even at great cost. They drove over a hundred miles to the examination centre in extreme heat and arrived just in time. The candidate rushed in, registered, and learned that Dr Willan was waiting for her. She played her first piece, still flustered about the trip and fear of being late.

Dad then said gently, "I think you can play better than that. I have an idea. Go and wash your hands and face. Take your time. I shall wait for you."

When she had finished her pieces, Dad told her that she had played so well he was going to give her very good marks. She cherished this memory all her life, being nervous and so in awe of the examiner and then having him treat her with such kindness and sensibility. I told her that her story reminded me so much of my father.

Index